Problems
in Form
and Function

language and being

edited by
George Lakoff
and
John Robert Ross

A. L. BECKER and ARAM A. YENGOYAN ● *The Imagination of Reality: Essays in Southeast Asian Coherence Systems,* 1979
WILLIAM E. COOPER ● *Speech Perception and Production: Studies in Selective Adaptation,* 1979
ANN BORKIN ● *Problems in Form and Function,* 1984

In Preparation

ANNALIESE KRAMER ● *The Languages of Linguistic Theory*
CHARLOTTE LINDE ● *The Creation of Coherence in Life Stories*
LIVIA POLANYI ● *The American Story*
JOHN ROBERT ROSS ● *Infinite Syntax*
TERRY WINOGRAD and FERNANDO FLORES ● *Understanding Cognition as Understanding*

Problems
in Form
and Function

Ann Borkin
University of Michigan

Ablex Publishing Corporation
Norwood, New Jersey 07648

Library of Congress Cataloging in Publication Data

Borkin, Ann.
    Problems in form and function.

    (The language and being series)
    Consists, in part, of the author's thesis (University of Michigan, 1974)
    Includes bibliographical references and index.
    1. English language—Clauses. 2. English language—Grammar, Generative.
I. Title. II. Series.
PE1385.B65 1982   425   82-11417
ISBN 0-89391-116-X

Ablex Publishing Corporation
355 Chestnut Street
Norwood, New Jersey 07648

Contents

Preface

Much of modern linguistics rests on the premise of *form/function duality:* that form is separate from, and independent of, function and content. In this view, form has its own structure and the relation between form and function is a matter of arbitrary convention. Saussure made that premise in his doctrine of the arbitrariness of the sign. Chomsky made the premise in his doctrine of the independence of syntax from semantics.

Ann Borkin's quiet book is as detailed a challenge as we know of to the premise of form/function quality. The detail and subtlety present in this work are of the greatest importance.

For subtlety, take two of the sentences Borkin discusses in Chapter Five:

(22) I find that this chair is uncomfortable.
(24) I find this chair uncomfortable.

She observes: "I might use (22), but not (24) as a statement about consumer reaction tests, but I would use (24) and not (22) as a statement about how the chair feels to me." Taken out of context, this might seem to be a random, isolated, and bizarre distinction. According to the premise of form/function quality, the relation between form, on the one hand, and function and content, on the other, is a matter of arbitrary convention. According to that premise, the facts might have been just the opposite.

By the time Borkin makes that observation in Chapter Five, however, she has shown that there is nothing arbitrary or random about this distinction. It is completely systematic and natural. The opposite could not occur. The principles by which form and function intertwine would not permit it. In such cases the relationship between form and function is *not* a matter *of arbitrary convention—it is a natural relationship.*

Many of us who have worked in the past twenty years on the shape of sentences have been content to, or have even had to, disregard many of the kinds of differences that are here the main focus of study. This disregarding—which one might wish to view as a justified idealization—has enabled the construction of a set of analytical tools of great power and beauty. While these tools are strong enough to tackle many problems of form, however, they are not sharp enough to disentangle the problems of function, and it is function to which the linguistics of the 1970's turned, on many fronts, with renewed interest.

The demonstration in this book of the inseparability and interdependence of form and function leaves us with an important challenge to our understanding of language: exactly what theory of language is necessary to account for the interdependencies of form and function that Borkin has uncovered? The depth of the problem is illustrated by Borkin's essay "Beheaded NP's". The examples she discusses there are known in the tradition of classical rhetoric as "metonymy". Linguists have generally ignored metonymy as a matter of pragmatics or language use—something independent of questions of linguistic form. In "Beheaded NP's", Borkin shows in overwhelming detail how metonymy intertwines with syntax. Her examples are dazzling and remain deep mysteries to this day. Such mysteries are central to our vision of what problems should be addressed by the linguistics of the 1980's and beyond. We are grateful for the gift of mysteries so worthy of the attention of those who would understand how language works.

George Lakoff
John Robert Ross

Acknowledgements

The monograph on raising to object position is my 1974 (University of Michigan) dissertation. It owes a great deal to John Lawler, who read and commented on every stage, and to George Lakoff, who has given me crucial training and support throughout my career in linguistics. I would also like to acknowledge the influence and support of Haj Ross. All three have been extremely generous with their friendship.

Finally, I would like to formally acknowledge here the influence of the work of Dwight Bolinger, although my admiration for his work will be evident throughout this volume.

I

Raising to Object Position: A Study in the Syntax and Semantics of Clause Merging

INTRODUCTION

In his 1974 monograph entitled *On Raising*, Paul Postal extensively motivated the existence of a transformational rule in English which has the effect of raising the subject of an object-embedded clause into object position of the matrix clause. According to this analysis, earlier proposed in Rosenbaum (1967) and Chomsky (1965), but challenged in Chomsky (1971), the italicized NP's in (1) and (2) following are subjects of embedded object clauses in underlying structure, but function in surface structure as objects of the matrix verbs *prove(s)* and *confirm(ed)*.

(1) That just proves *Susan* to be a poor risk.
(2) Fred confirmed *there* to be too many onlookers.

The exact formulation of a rule of Raising depends a great deal upon the particular theoretical framework the rule is to be fitted to. So, for instance, in the framework Rosenbaum was working in, Raising to object position (Rosenbaum's "Pronoun Replacement") operated on the output of Extraposition, the raised subject replacing an *it* stranded after Extraposition has made the complement S a daughter of the matrix VP. This raising operation is schematized in (3), an arrow marking the path of movement of the complement subject and the deletion of *it* symbolized by a crossmark.

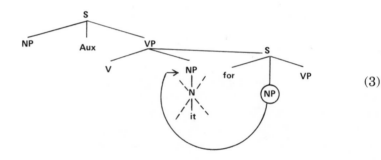

(3)

In a Generative Semantics framework with verb-initial underlying order, such as that proposed in McCawley (1970), Raising to object position is one aspect of a more general rule of Raising schematized in (4).

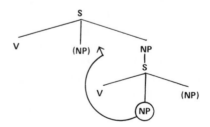

(4)

Postal's motivation for and characterization of Raising will be valid in other frameworks, as well, although the rule will be formulated still differently in these.

For the purposes of this study I will schematize the operation of Raising to object position as in (5), which contains the lexical items needed for the derivation of (2).

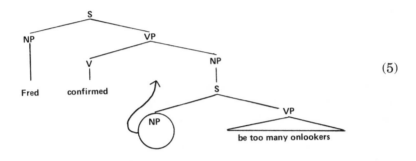

(5)

Postal's arguments that Raising does not operate on the output of Extraposition are reflected in (5). I use a constituent structure and node labeling close to that of Standard theory because it will be the most familiar to the largest number of readers, not because I espouse the particular theory of grammar associated with a structure like that in (5). For the same reason, the discussion in this monograph will be carried out largely in the vocabulary of Standard theory, although it can be translated into the vocabularies of other current theoretical frameworks. The problems discussed in this work do not arise from one particular theory and are relevant to any theory which counts as part of its scope the systematic facts about English examined here.

Sentences like (1) and (2) with infinitive complements can be contrasted with sentences like (6) and (7), with *that* clauses as object complements.

(1) That just proves *Susan* to be a poor risk.
(2) Fred confirmed *there* to be too many onlookers.
(6) That just proves that *Susan* is a poor risk.
(7) Fred confirmed that *there* were too many onlookers.

The *that* clauses in (6) and (7) represent underlying object complements undisturbed by Raising, the italicized NP's continuing to function in surface structure as subjects of object complements.

The Raising analysis of infinitives like those in (1) and (2) is a contemporary attempt to deal with facts often noticed by earlier grammarians: 1) that, logically, the italicized constituents in both (1) and (2), and (6) and (7), function as subjects of object complements: 2) that, however, nominal constituents in pre-infinitive position like those italicized in (1) and (2) have grammatical characteristics of objects of the main verb rather than subjects of the complement.

Sentences with infinitives like those in (1) and (2) have often been contrasted with superficially similar sentences like those in (8) and (9).

(8) Jack persuaded *me* to give up coffee.
(9) They forced *Harry* to hand over the keys.

Generally, it has been agreed that sentences like (8) and (9) differ from those like (1) and (2) in that the nominal constituent after the main verb is logically an argument of it, the *to* infinitive serving both logically and grammatically as an adjunct to this primary relationship (cf. Poutsma, chapter XVIII, and Jespersen, chapter LV). Rosenbaum continues this tradition by analyzing the italicized NP's in (8) and (9) as objects in underlying structure which act as controllers in a rule of Equi NP Deletion removing the coreferential subject of the complement. The operation of Equi NP Deletion is schematized in (10), which contains the lexical items necessary for the derivation of (9).

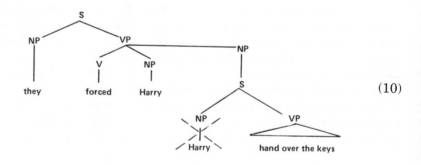

(10)

In this study I will generally not question Rosenbaum's analysis, although it has since been challenged on several grounds; for instance, Jackendoff (1972) formulates Equi as a rule of semantic interpretation rather than a syntactic deletion rule, and Postal (1973) suggests that many verbs heretofore regarded as Equi-governing may in fact govern Raising. I think my using Rosenbaum's analysis is legitimate here, since, on the one hand, the discussion can be translated into Jackendoff's framework, and on the other hand, I will be concerned primarily with verbs that most clearly govern Raising—that is, with proposition-embedding verbs (Postal's B Verbs) like *believe, prove, announce, consider*, etc. Although Postal's suggestion of a Raising analysis for verbs that have been treated as governing Equi is certainly relevant to the general topic of constraints on Raising to object position, B Verbs do not figure very strongly in Postal's proposal (but see my Chapter VI).

To repeat some essentials, then, although sentences with Raising-derived infinitives like (1) and (2) are superficially more like sentences with apparently Equi-derived infinitives like (8) and (9), their logical similarity to sentences with *that* clauses as surface structure objects has long been recognized and is not challenged today. Since Chomsky has recently challenged the surface structure object status of pre-*to* NP's in sentences like (1) and (2), the primary thrust of Postal's (1974) study is toward presenting a large, varied, and hopefully incontrovertible body of evidence for the derived object status of these preinfinitival NP's. In the present study, I will assume that Postal has achieved his goal; that is, I will assume that the NP's in question are indeed derived objects. I will also assume that the discrepancy between the surface structure *Subject Verb Object (subjectless clause)* organization of sentences like (1) and (2) and the more logically revealing *Subject Verb (full clause)* organization is to be reflected by a rule of Raising to object position, which raises an underlying subject of an embedded clause into object position of the matrix clause.

In the following chapters, I intend to examine the relation of syntactic, semantic and pragmatic constraints on Raising to object position to the surface structure syntactic results of that rule, which partially merges two underlying clauses into one clause in surface structure. I will limit my investigation primarily to English constructions of four types: 1) sentences with *that* clauses functioning as objects; 2) sentences with infinitives derived by Raising, with no other rule further breaking up the underlying object clause; 3) sentences with infinitives derived by Raising that are further broken up by *to be* Deletion, as in (11);

(11a) I consider Jean to be obnoxious.
(11b) I consider Jean obnoxious.

and 4) sentences with as + gerund constructions that I will argue are also derived by Raising to object position, sentences like those in (12) and (13).

(12) I regard Jean as being obnoxious.
(13) We've established Harry as having been the primary instigator of the insurrection.

I will also limit the investigation to verbs that embed clauses describing propositions (*believe, prove, announce, reveal*, etc.) rather than verbs that embed clauses describing anticipated events or states of affairs (*expect, allow, want, need*, etc.). The proposition-embedding verbs (Postal's B Verbs) occur more readily with *that* clauses and *as* constructions, while the other group mentioned (Postal's W Verbs) differ from these proposition-embedding verbs in enough other ways to warrant separate study.

The next chapter contains support for Postal's suggestion that some *as* + gerund constructions are to be derived by Raising. In the third chapter, I argue that although NP's in both pre-*as* + gerund position and pre-*to* infinitive position are objects in surface structure, SVO strings before *as* show a greater degree of syntactic integrity than do SVO strings before *to*. In short, raised objects in *as* constructions behave slightly more like objects than do raised objects in infinitive constructions; for in some very subtle ways, subjectless infinitive adjuncts still function with their erstwhile subjects as embedded object clauses, while subjectless gerundive adjuncts with *as* function in such strings slightly more like adverbials.

In Chapter IV, I examine semantic characteristics of constructions derived by Raising to object position. I show that the syntactic process of merging two separate underlying clauses into a surface structure *SVO + Adjunct* string accompanies a tendency for the underlying complement to be viewed as characterizing or making a judgment about a specific object or person rather than viewed more objectively as an empirically oriented description of an event or state of affairs. Predictably, the greater surface structure integrity of derived SVO strings with *as* constructions discussed in Chapter III parallels an increased strictness in semantic and pragmatic constraints on Raising-derived *as* constructions.

In Chapter V, I examine constraints on *to be* Deletion and *that* Deletion, both of which, it is argued, have the effect of weakening the separate clause status of an underlying object complement. It is again argued that this surface structure effect is related to constraints on the operation of these two rules, which constraints are similar to constraints on Raising to object position.

Chapter VI contains an examination of some problems with deciding non-arbitrarily which SVO + adjunct strings are to be derived by removing the subject of the adjunct clause by Raising and which are to be derived by removing the subject not by Raising but by a deletion rule. An alternative to the Equi vs. Raising analysis in which such problems arise is briefly sketched in this chapter. Chapter VII contains concluding remarks.

There is a great deal of idiolectal variation in acceptability judgments about Raising-derived sentences. This variation is evident with regard to what verbs govern Raising, what kind of constituent can be raised, and what kind of complement can be broken up by Raising. I have found people who are very free in accepting Raising-derived examples, as well as people for whom most of the sentences in this monograph are at least slightly strange. Even constraints on Raising for a single informant will vary in strictness according to what verb is involved. Readers at either end of the spectrum will be in a state of discomfort, for it is annoying to follow a discussion based on distinctions between sentences one either finds all quite respectable or, worse, all pretty bad.

The discussion will be concerned with the relative merits of relevant sentences rather than absolute judgments as marked, however. For instance, while all of the sentences in (14) are derived from structures with object complements, sentences like those in (14) can be placed on a surface structure one clause-two clause continuum, sentences with *that* clauses behaving most like they contain two separate clauses in surface structure, and sentences with *to be* Deletion behaving most like one surface structure clause (Ross, 1972b).

(14a) I believe that Jim is self-serving.
(14b) I believe Jim is self-serving.
(14c) I consider Jim to be self-serving.
(14d) I consider Jim self-serving.

In order to show that constraints on what kind of NP can be found in a position immediately after the main verb are related to where the construction in question falls on a one clause-two clause continuum, for instance, it is not necessary that everyone agree with the markings on individual sentences; rather, what is necessary is to show that no matter what the individual judgments on particular sentences are, speakers share a tendency to be stricter for constructions more like one surface structure clause, and more lenient for those more like two clauses in surface structure. Although not everyone will agree with how I've marked the sentences in (15), if a particular speaker accepts one of the sentences in (15), he or she should accept all of the sentences before it on the list, and if a speaker finds one of the sentences unacceptable or strange, he or she should find all others after it to be equally bad or worse. Cutoff points for acceptability judgments will vary from speaker to speaker, but the general tendency should be the same.

(15a) He believes that the littlest movement is threatening to him.

(15b) (?) He believes the littlest movement is threatening to him.
(15c) ? He believes the littlest movement to be threatening to him.
(15d) *He believes the littlest movement threatening to him.

Generally, the individual markings on sentences in this work will reflect a very conservative view of my own judgments, since I started out with a relatively liberal Raising pattern and now find my judgments to be liberal to the point of near-anarchy.

The challenge of this kind of orderly variation has not yet been satisfactorily met in current generative theory, although I am indebted to Ross's lead in bringing it out and inspecting it. With regard to the data discussed in this study, the extreme amount of variation has made it impossible to honestly formulate any neat, formal and elegant Principles or Constraints; rather, I must rely on more humble observations of "tendencies" and informal generalizations which, I believe, are still interesting and valid, for all their inelegance.

II

As Constructions and Raising

In order to show that Raising to Object Position has operated to derive a particular construction, it is necessary to show both: 1) that a putatively raised constituent functions as an object in a matrix clause at some non-initial point in the derivation of the construction, and 2) that the constituent in question does not originate in object position, but rather functions as subject of an embedded clause at some more remote point in the derivation. Since the underlying subject status of pre-*to* NP's in putatively Raising-derived infinitives has not been questioned, the heaviest artillery in Postal 1974 is aimed at establishing the derived object status of these NP's. For the constructions discussed in this chapter, however, the situation is reversed. No one challenges the object status of the italicized pre-*as* NP's in sentences like (1–11); rather, the problem is to show that these NP's do not originate in their surface structure object position.

(1) Fran immediately recognized *Joan's odd behavior* as being a ploy to detract attention from Harry.

(2) Since I didn't know anything about Sam firsthand, I just accepted *him* as being the fool that John said he was.

(3) Mary won't admit *Jim's presence* as being at all unnerving to her.

(4) Hal's sister views *his playing rugby* as being a good way to release pent up aggression.

(5) Marv perceived *it* as being too late to make amends.

(6) Lorraine sees *this* as being her big chance to make it as a stripper.

(7) The referee has declared *the grassy area* as being out of bounds only for the girls with the red pinnies.

(8) CBS reports *Anderson and Hocksmith* as having been the first over the finish line.

(9) Further investigation will reveal *the land* as being worth more than you think.

(10) I regard *your suggestion* as being totally inappropriate.

(11) His actions have already established *the defendant* as being extremely volatile under pressure.

In all of these sentences, the missing subject of the post *as* gerund is coreferential with the object of the matrix verb. In the framework I am working in, the missing subject can have been removed in one of several ways; either it has been removed by Raising from a structure like that in (12);

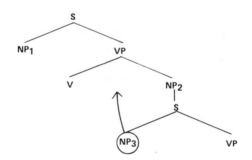

(12)

or it has been deleted by standard Equi NP Deletion or a similar deletion rule from a structure like that in (13):

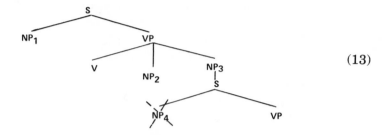

(13)

or it has been deleted by an Equi-like rule from some unknown kind of structure, as schematized in (14), a structure in which the gerundive

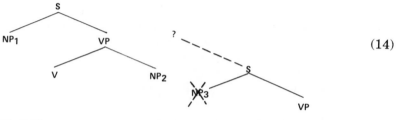

(14)

$NP_2 = NP_3$

clause does not originate as an object complement of the matrix verb. A Raising analysis, then, competes with a regular Equi analysis, and two Equi-like analyses.[1]

I think we can eliminate the Equi-like analysis from a mystery source schematized in (14), because if *as* gerunds like those in (1–11) do not originate as object complements, but as some other, more adverbial or subordinate clause-like source, we would expect the pre-*as* SVO string to represent a propositional unit that is modified or expanded on in some way by the *as* clause. This is in fact the case for many *as* constructions that are not putatively derived by Raising; in each of the sentences in (15–23), for instance, the italicized main clause Subject Verb Object string represents an isolable assertion that is qualified or expanded on by the *as* phrase that follows.

(15) *Mamie refused the medicine* as a deliberate challenge to the nurse's authority.

(16) *Sue made an umbrella stand* as a token of her respect.

(17) *Mabel welcomed Sam's departure* as an excuse to go bananas.

(18) *Mabel loves John* as a mother, but as a voter she distrusts him.

(19) *Frank admitted Murphy* as a friend of the groom, although strictly speaking he shouldn't have been at the wedding at all.

(20) *Peebles assassinated Fitzhugh* as a last-ditch attempt to achieve notoriety.

(21) *Sally ate a lot of chili* as a child.

(22) *Frank rejected the hamburger* as being too greasy, but he accepted the french fries.

(23) *Max introduced Harry* as the world's greatest frogman.

In contrast to these, the SVO strings in the sentences in (1–11) do not represent assertions that are interpretable in isolation in exactly the same way as they are when the *as* clause is added. Although (23) entails that Max introduced Harry, for instance, (10) *(Further investigation will reveal the land as being worth more than you think)* does not entail *Further investigation will reveal the land.* The *as* constructions that I will regard as putatively Raising-derived will be of the kind in which the surface-structure main clause SVO string is *not* independently assertable with the same reading as it has with an *as* clause following it. The problem, then, is to determine whether SVO strings like those in (1–11) are derived by Raising, or by regular Equi NP Deletion or an another, probably *ad hoc,* deletion rule removing the subject of an object complement.

Syntactic motivation for a Raising analysis of *as* constructions is hard to come by. It was Postal who first suggested a Raising analysis of such constructions, admitting the paucity of syntactic argumentation for this position; and where Postal fails to find syntactic argumentation, it is certain that the syntactic pickings are slim. In fact, even a "consideration not without relevance" presented by Postal turns out not to have any force in this matter.

Postal's consideration is this: he states that in cases where a Raising analysis is unquestioned, as in (24) and (25) (Postal's [105a] and [105b]) there is an emphatic reflexive floating into the complement, while in unquestioned Equi cases, as in (26) and (27) (Postal's [106a] and [106b]), emphatic reflexives don't float into the Equi'd complement. (The acceptability judgments of [24–27] are Postal's.)

(24)   Jack seems to have himself called Sylvia.

(25)   Jason appears unlikely to himself finish first.

(26)   *Jack wants to himself call Sylvia.

(27)   *Harry expects to have himself moved by then.

Postal states that emphatic reflexives do float into *as* clauses, as in (28–30) (Postal's [106c–106e]). (Again, the judgments are Postal's.)

(28) Jack strikes me as having himself over-estimated the opposition.

(29) I regard Jack as being unlikely to himself visit that commune.

(30) I regard Jack as having himself violated our agreement.

If the correct generalization is that emphatic reflexives float into only those clauses whose subject has been removed by Raising, then (28–30) are evidence for Raising-derived *as* clauses. However, I doubt that this is the correct generalization, since for me (25) and (29) are questionable sentences, and I find (31) and (32), with emphatic reflexives in *as* clauses quite clearly not derived by Raising, better than (29).

(31) John introduced Mary as being likely to herself run for governor.

(32) ?Senator Bland resigned as being himself too involved in the Nusbaum affair to be of any help to the committee.

Other speakers I have consulted dislike all of (24), (25), (29), and, to a lesser degree, (30), as well as my sentences (31) and (32), so if there is an argument here for Raising it will have to be rescued by Postal or someone else with a great deal of ingenuity.

The most widely acceptable kind of evidence possible for the underlying subject status of pre-*as* NP's is the presence in pre-*as* position of non-referential *it* and nonreferential NP idiom chunks like *the cat, the shit,* and *the ice* in idioms like *let the cat out of the bag, the shit hit the fan,* and *break the ice.*[2] Although the occurrence of such non-referential NP's in pre-*as* position is much more strictly limited than their occurrence in pre-*to* position, I have found no one who objects to the following sentences:

(33) Joan immediately recognized it as being much too late to make an effective countermove.

(34) I regard it as being muggy, but Sam thinks it's just pleasantly damp.

(35) I saw it as being too late to apologize.

(36) I perceived it as being foggy out in the pastures, but Frank told me that the illusion was created by his new XBXX machine.

(37) Mary viewed it as being too late to even try to get gas.

Postal quotes Ross as offering these two:

(38) I regard it as being foggy enough to cover our retreat.
(39) He recognizes it as being too windy to sail.

Sentences (40–46) are sentences for which I have found widespread but not total acceptance. I expect that many people who will accept (33–39) will hesitate at (40–46).

(40) Robert acknowledged it as being rather late in the evening to go out for pizza, but he said he was hungry enough to try.
(41) Frank mistakenly perceived the ice as having been broken already and got out his clarinet.
(42) I perceived the shit as being about to hit the fan, but Martha told me not worry.
(43) The flight expert has just reported it as being too muggy for the engine to operate.
(44) They haven't yet established it as having rained at all on the night of the murder.
(45) We've established the shit as having hit the fan well before election day.
(46) Our inquiries have revealed it as not always being pleasant in Monte Carlo.

Sentences (47–49) also have some admirers, but my impression is that more people will balk at these than at the sentences above.

(47) Our research has confirmed it as being measurably hotter during this decade than during the last.
(48) The jury just accepted it as having rained on the night of the murder.
(49) He will never admit it as being windier on the porch now than it was before he built the screen.

The force of these examples as evidence for a Raising analysis lies in the nature of Equi NP Deletion and assumptions about the distribution in underlying structure of non-referential NP's like *it* in weather, distance and time expressions, non-deictic *there,* and NP's that are parts of idioms. Postal (1974) has a complete and concise account of the reasoning behind such arguments. To summarize briefly here, Equi NP Deletion deletes an NP under coreference with another NP, and so a regular Equi NP Deletion analysis is not possible for sentences with non-referential NP's in object position like those in

(33–49); rather, an *ad hoc* extension of Equi would be required to derive such sentences. Also, the occurrence of *it* used in weather, distance and time expressions, and NP idiom chunks (Postal's terminology), has long been argued to be constrained in underlying structure; their presence in surface structure as objects, only when there is an infinitive or *as* clause containing the rest of the weather or time expression, or the rest of the idiom, would follow from an analysis in which they either originally occurred in underlying structure in their normal position, or are inserted into their normal position during the course of a derivation, but in any case are removed from that position by a Raising rule.

The evidence given in examples (33–49) above would be more impressive if non-referential NP's occurred more freely in pre-*as* position. However, such examples virtually clinch a Raising analysis in some instances, and since non-referential NP's traditionally serve as "tracers" for a more generally applicable movement rule, there is reason to believe that Postal is right in suggesting that Raising derives *as* constructions as well as infinitives. In the next two chapters, I will argue that the fact that "empty" NP's occur with overwhelmingly less frequency with *as* constructions than with infinitives is related to the fact that the surface structure syntactic integrity of SVO strings is greater with *as* constructions than with infinitives, which in some very subtle ways still function with their former subjects like embedded object clauses rather than like subjectless adverbial adjuncts.

Before I leave the non-referential NP argument, I would like to call attention to a few sentences volunteered and vouched for by Stacy Krainz.

(50) I $\begin{Bmatrix} \text{acknowledge} \\ \text{regard} \end{Bmatrix}$ there as being a real problem with security on campus.

(51) I view there as being a lack of self-control among college students.

Most people I have talked with would award these sentences with a triple star for awfulness, although several people have commented that they are "not as bad as they should be," or that they might say them but would never write them; and in fact I have found one other person who likes them. I leave them here as a stunning reminder of the extremes of syntactic variation and as one more scrap of evidence for a rule of Raising deriving *as* constructions.

If the *as* constructions in question in this chapter were to be derived by deletion out of an object complement, a like object-subject constraint on the order of that proposed for Equi-governing infinitive constructions in Perlmutter (1971) would have to be operative to ensure that the object NP of the matrix clause is in some relevant sense identical to the subject NP of the complement. The identity involved would not be the coreference required for an Equi NP Deletion analysis of infinitive constructions like those in (52) and (53);

> (52) Fran forced Mary to confess.
> (53) John tried to extinguish the fire.

for not only does non-referential *it* occur as pre-*as* object, but gerundive complements occur in this position, too, as in (54–56).

> (54) John regarded Harry's cracking up on Tuesday as being the final link in a long chain of events.
> (55) Myrtle views Tom's shooting pigeons as being a harmless pastime that he'll grow out of sooner or later.
> (56) We've established Mary's winning the gold cup as bothering Jim more than her wearing his tennis shorts.

That is, the needed like object-subject constraint and the concomitant identity conditions for deletion would not be the same as those needed for constructions involving regular Equi. Cases of regular Equi out of object complements typically involve coreference between two NP's referring to the same volitional being. (In 53–56), the relevant NP's do not represent beings or even objects, but rather are clauses functioning as NP's. In the following sentences, the pre-*as* NP's represent abstractions rather than materially existing objects or people.

> (57) I view physical beauty as being a liability in certain cases.
> (58) The inquiry revealed financial gain as being Harry's strongest motive.

In summary, then, if the *as* constructions discussed here are to be derived by a deletion rule rather than by Raising, this deletion rule does not have the same identity conditions as regular Equi NP Deletion.

There is a semantic argument for Raising in the style of Postal (1970), that also has to do with the nature of the identity between the two NP's that would be involved in the deletion rule necessary under a non-Raising analysis. This argument concerns metonymous NP's, or "beheaded NP's," as they are referred to elsewhere in this volume. The underlined NP's in the following (a) sentences are metonymous NP's;

their semantic content is made explicit by the fuller NP's underlined in the (b) sentences.

(59a) *IBM* dropped ten points in one day.
(59b) *The price of IBM stock* dropped ten points in one day.
(60a) *Nixon* was secretly bombing Cambodia in 1970.
(60b) *U. S. troops under the control of Nixon* were secretly bombing Cambodia in 1970.
(61a) *Brian* is too small to impress the jocks in the locker room.
(61b) $\begin{cases} Brian\text{'}s\ penis \\ Brian\text{'}s\ body \end{cases}$ is too small to impress the jocks in the locker room.

Rules demanding coreference between two NP's do not always demand what I will call "strict" coreference; that is, they do not always require that two metonymous NP's refer to exactly the same entity. Equi NP Deletion does not demand strict coreference; for instance, in (62) it is Maisie's breasts that fit into a brassiere, but it is some other aspect of Maisie that thinks or wants; and in one reading of (63), Nixon is not threatening to himself bomb Havana[3] but rather is threatening to send representatives of the U.S. government to do the bombing. Equi in these cases is oblivious to such semantic distinctions.

(62) Maisie wants to fit into a C cup.
(63) Nixon is threatening to bomb Havana.

I've previously argued that the *as* constructions whose derivation is in question here aren't derived by regular Equi, because any deletion rule operating in the derivation of such *as* constructions would not demand the same type of coreference as does Equi. I've observed that such a rule would have weaker constraints on identity, treating as identical two instances of weather *it,* of the same NP idiom chunks, of the same NP complements, and of NP's not referring to objects in the material world. In view of this, it would be a totally *ad hoc* and unexpected characteristic of such a deletion rule that it should demand strict coreference between metonymous NP's. And, apparently, this would be the case in an Equi-like analysis; for I have found no instances of putatively Raising-derived *as* constructions in which the missing NP subject of the gerund is not strictly coreferential with the superficial pre-*as* object. This would be expected in a Raising analysis, which involves only one occurrence of the NP in question, but it would be extremely suspicious in an Equi-like analysis. Supporting examples with strict coreferentiality are found in (64–69).

(64a)   Maxine regards Robert as being too small for her to brag
          about.

(64a = b) Maxine regards Robert's penis as being too small for her
          to brag about.

(65a)   I've no doubt that further investigation will reveal IBM
          as being worth a lot more than is suspected.

(65a = b) I've no doubt that further investigation will reveal IBM
          stock as being worth a lot more than is suspected.

(66a)   We've established Tom as being the larger of the two.

(66a = b) We've established Tom's $\begin{Bmatrix} \text{penis} \\ \text{body} \end{Bmatrix}$ as being the larger of the two.

(67a)   Nader reports Bell Tel as being solely responsible for the
          brownout.

(67a = b) Nader reports
          $\begin{Bmatrix} \text{the executives at Bell Tel} \\ \text{the physical apparatus of Bell Tel} \end{Bmatrix}$
          as being solely responsible for the brownout.

(68a)   Barker perceived Havana as being the foremost threat
          to the security of the US

(68a = b) Barker perceived the government centered in Havana as
          being the foremost threat to the security of the US.

(69a)   After ten silicone injections, Dr. Mammary has finally
          proclaimed Mary as being big enough to qualify for his
          Star Bosom Certificate.

(69a = b) After ten silicone injections, Dr. Mammary has finally
          proclaimed Mary's breasts as being big enough to qualify
          for his Star Bosom Certificate.

Examples (70–73) contrast with the examples above in that they
show loose coreferentiality in sentences with *as* constructions that I
have not been characterizing as putatively derived by Raising.

(70a)   I recognize that man as having weighed more than me
          yesterday at the weigh-in.

(70a ≠ b) I recognize that man's body as having weighed more than
          me yesterday at the weigh-in.

(71a)   The M. C. introduced Mick Jagger as being large enough
          to amaze the most jaded of groupies.

(71a ≠ b) The M. C. introduced Mick Jagger's penis as being large
          enough to amaze the most jaded of groupies.

(72a)   The novel characterizes King Rudolph as constantly in-
          vading foreign countries.

(72a ≠ b) The novel characterizes King Rudolph's army as constantly invading foreign countries.

Since Rosenbaum (1967), one way of discriminating verbs that govern Equi NP Deletion from verbs that govern Raising is to compare variants in which Passive has and has not applied in the complement. If such variants differ truth-functionally, by some informal notion of truth functional equivalence, the verb is classified as an Equi-governing verb, since only an Equi NP Deletion analysis entails that these variants would differ in underlying structure (that is, differ in a way not linked to the application of Passive). For instance, an Equi NP Deletion analysis of sentences with infinitives like those in (73) would derive the (a) variant from a structure in which *Horace* would be an underlying direct object of *persuade,* and the b variant from a structure in which *Mr. Paul* occupies underlying object position.

(73a) Bill encouraged Horace to be made up by Mr. Paul.
(73b) Bill encouraged Mr. Paul to make up Horace.

A Raising analysis, the standard argument goes, would provide no basis for the difference apparent in (73). The variants in (73) would differ only in that Passive has applied in (73a); but Passive does not normally accompany a truth-functional difference. The lack of a truth functional meaning difference in variants like those in (74), on the other hand, would be expected in a regular (pre-Postal and pre-Lakoff) Raising analysis but not in an Equi NP Deletion analysis.

(74a) Bill considers Horace to have been made up masterfully by Mr. Paul.
(74b) Bill considers Mr. Paul to have made up Horace masterfully.

Postal has recently challenged the assumption that a truth-functional difference in meaning is motivation for an Equi NP Deletion analysis; he suggests that such differences in meaning may be represented by the linking of speaker assumptions to Raising, rather than by the presence of extra NP's in underlying structure. Under such an analysis, then, all the sentences in (73) and (74) could be derived by Raising, the differences in (73) being linked to speaker assumptions about who took the initiative of accomplishing the action described in the complement.

If Postal is correct, and the lack of truth-functional equivalence of active and passive variants does not disconfirm a Raising analysis,

I think it's still true that the fact of truth-functional equivalence supports a Raising analysis. For if variants that do not differ truth-functionally were to be derived from different underlying structures, as would be the case in a non-Raising analysis of *as* constructions in sentences like those in (75–79) below, some kind of principle would have to be stated that would guarantee the lack of semantic import of an extra occurrence of the object NP's in such sentences.

(75a)   Jacob refuses to recognize his stubborness as having completely ruined our cause.

(75a = b) Jacob refuses to recognize our cause as having been completely ruined by his stubborness.

(76a)   The news agency confirmed the airplane as having been completely destroyed by the hijackers.

(76a = b) The news agency confirmed the hijackers as having completely destroyed the airplane.

(77a)   Our inquiry has finally established the old lady as having been stabbed by the nephew with a small pair of sewing scissors.

(77a = b) Our inquiry has finally established the nephew as having stabbed the old lady with a small pair of sewing scissors.

(78a)   I regard Mary as having in effect abandoned Sam.

(78a = b) I regard Sam as having in effect been abandoned by Mary.

(79a)   Maxine perceives Pat as having encouraged Jacob.

(79a = b) Maxine perceives Jacob as having been encouraged by Pat.

The lack of truth-functional meaning differences in the variants in (75–79) would be predicted by a Raising analysis, however.

Chomsky (1971) presented an argument against Raising to Object Position that has since been refuted by Bresnan (1972) and Postal (1974). Chomsky observed that NP's can be questioned from *of* genitives with picture nouns if the picture noun is in object position, as in (80b), but not if the picture noun is in subject position, as in (81b).

(80a)   John paints pictures of Mao in his spare time.

(80b)   Who does John paint pictures of in his spare time?

(81a)   Pictures of Mao are said to shed tears of May Day.

(81b)   *Who are pictures of said to shed tears on May Day?

He also observed that NP's can't be questioned from picture noun *of* genitives that are in what traditionally has been assumed to be object position before infinitives, as in (82b).

(82a)   John believes pictures of Mao to be sacrosanct.

(82b)   ?*What famous leader does John believe pictures of to be sacrosanct?

He concluded that such NP's aren't in fact in object position in surface structure but still function as subjects of infinitive clause.

Bresnan points out that NP's can't be questioned from certain picture noun *of* genitives that are in pre-*as* position, either, and gives the following example:

(83)   *What kind of actress does he regard pictures of as a form of exploitation?

She concludes that since pre-*as* NP's are unquestionably surface objects, Chomsky's argument has no force.

Postal's reply to Chomsky's picture noun argument is this: the constraint is *not* that NP's can be questioned from picture noun *of* genitives only if the picture noun isn't in subject position at the point in the derivation when the question rule applies; rather, the appropriate constraint is that NP's can't be questioned from picture noun *of* genitives if the picture noun is a cyclic subject—by Postal's definition of cyclic subject, if the picture noun has a corresponding constituent NP which is the subject of a clause at the end of some cycle. If Postal's formulation of the constraint is correct, then, the similarity in behavior that Bresnan noticed (between genitives of picture nouns in object position before infinitives and those in object position with *as* constructions) is an argument for the cyclic subject status of pre-*as* picture nouns whose genitives can't be questioned.

Postal himself casts doubt on whether his formulation of the constraint is correct; he quotes Kuno, McCawley, and Ross as challenging the claim that the relevant generalization involves the notion of subject (cyclic or otherwise). Further complication is brought to the issue by widespread idiolectal variation with regard to the data involved. For instance, I have found that some speakers will accept sentences like (83), and (84).

(84)   What kind of actress does he consider pictures of to be a form of exploitation?

Where a complex NP with a picture noun *of* genitive is an object, I have found only this generalization to hold across variation: the more easily the *Subject Verb Object* string can be interpreted as an independent assertion followed by an adjunct qualifying it, the more easily it can be questioned out of.

As an example of this, I give the sentences in (85) and (86).

(85a) John allowed pictures of Linda Lovelace to be circulated among the students.

(85b) Who did John allow pictures of to be circulated among the students?

(86a) John allowed pictures of Linda Lovelace to be destroyed by the censors.

(86b) Who did John allow pictures of to be destroyed by the censors?

Most people will dislike both (85b) and (86b). However, I predict that more people will approve of (85b) than of (86b), and that many people will judge (85b) as better than (86b). The reason is, I believe, that in (85a), the SVO string, *John allowed pictures of Linda Lovelace*, is meaningful in itself and is not contradicted but expanded on by the rest of the infinitive clause; while in (86a), the same SVO string interpreted in isolation runs counter to the sentence as a whole. If this is an accurate description of the facts, then the kind of information needed to state the relevant constraint on Question Formation not only has to do with the logical structure of a derived string rather than with purely syntactic information, but it has to do with the logical structure of a derived string that is not even a constituent in surface structure. Another such case is discussed in Bolinger (1967b) and will be taken up in Chapter VI of this work; for the purposes of this chapter, I will only repeat what apparently is necessary in evaluating the result of questioning out of picture noun *of*-genitives: 1) a string that is derived, and not even a constituent in surface structure must be referred to; 2) whether or not this string is separately derivable as a meaningful sentence of English must be determined; 3) if the string is separately derivable, the meaning of the independently derived sentence and of the whole sentence of which the non-constituent string is a part must be compatible, in a sense I will try to sharpen later with regard to other constructions.

Similar examples can be found with *as* constructions. Matthew Dryer has volunteered (87b) as acceptable to him:

(87a) They regard pictures of lizards as being acceptable gifts.[4]

(87b) What kind of animals do they regard pictures of as being acceptable gifts?

Certainly, not everyone will agree that (87b) is good; I think that (88b) will be consistently judged as worse, however, for people who can discriminate between the two.

(88a) The experts have established pictures of lizards as being disturbing to small children.
(88b) What kind of animals have the experts established pictures of as being disturbing to small children?

Notice that the SVO string in (87a) can be used (comparatively) independently, as in (89), but that the same is not true of the SVO string in (38).

(89) Q. How do they regard pictures of lizards?
      A. As being acceptable, but not desirable.
(90) *Q. How have they established pictures of lizards?
      A. As being disturbing to small children.

The relevance of these facts to a Raising analysis is that one would expect the semantic and syntactic integrity of SVO strings that are derived by Raising to be less than that of SVO strings that are not derived. The results of questioning of picture noun *of* genitives with *as* constructions is consistent with a Raising analysis of some of these constructions and a non-Raising analysis of others. That is, the sentences putatively derived by Raising resist such questioning, while those not claimed to be so derived, do not.

(91)   (putatively Raising-derived *as* constructions)
(91a) *Which positions does Greg refuse to recognize descriptions of as being relevant?
(91b) *Which guru have they revealed pictures of as having been on the wall at the time of the explosion?
(91c) ?Who does Jack view posters of as being in bad taste?
(92)   (*as* constructions not claimed to be derived by Raising)
(92a) What kind of animals do they use pictures of as decoration?
(92b) Who would you describe pictures of as being slightly titillating?
(92c) What kind of activity do they destroy movies of, as being unsuitable for home viewing?

All these facts certainly don't amount to a spectacular argument for Raising, but I think they are relevant.

I have presented the case for Raising to Object Position deriving some *as* constructions. Essentially, motivation for this analysis rests on a rejection of both an analysis in which they arise from object complements through regular NP Deletion (or an *ad hoc* deletion rule) and an analysis in which these *as* constructions are underlying adverbial-like adjuncts modifying a basic assertion carried by the SVO string. *As* constructions that I have considered not to be putatively derived by Raising are of the latter type; that is, these *as* constructions do function as an expansion of or qualification on basic SVO strings, and the missing subjects of these *as* gerunds, however they are removed, do not seem to be removed by regular Equi in that they do not have to be referential in the sense of referring to an entity or object.

In any construction derived by Raising to Object Position, I believe, there is a tension between the surface structure syntactic integrity of the derived SVO string and the more logically revealing underlying constituent structure that I schematize as *SV (Clause)*. I think that the tension is greater in the case of *as* constructions; I will argue in the next chapter that the surface structure syntactic integrity of the SVO string with such constructions is greater than that of corresponding strings with infinitive constructions, and in Chapter VI I will show that the either-or distinction between an Equi or Equi-like analysis and a Raising analysis is often difficult to sustain. In this chapter, we have already seen at least one instance in which what I will now assume to be a Raising-governing verb, *regard*, functions as main verb in a sentence that seems to be both basically and superficially of the *SVO (adverbial adjunct)* type. I repeat the relevant examples here for convenience.

(89)   Q. How do they regard pictures of lizards?
        A. As being acceptable, but not desirable.
(87a)   They regard pictures of lizards as being acceptable gifts.

Notice that *regard* behaves more like the Raising verb I claim it is, in 93 and 94

(93)   Q. How do they regard Max?
       *A. As having insulted Mary.
(94a)   They regard Max as having insulted Mary.
(94a = b)   They regard Mary as having been insulted by Max.

In brief, then, we are dealing with the same kind of non-discrete phenomenon long recognized by more traditional grammarians, who felt free to make such statements as "the degree of connection between the accusative and infinitive varies" (Meyer-Myklestad), "these classes pass imperceptibly into one another" (Jespersen), and "It will now be seen that the construction of (39a) occupies a position midway between that of (39b) and (41)" (Zandvoort). (These statements all concern infinitive constructions.) I believe that such statements do not necessarily betray inaccuracies or weaknesses in the analysis of the data, and that in the case of the constructions discussed here, they represent accurate descriptions of the facts. How to give a formal interpretation of these facts is a different matter, and will be touched on at the end of the next chapter.

CHAPTER II FOOTNOTES

[1]In a framework such as that suggested in Postal (1974) and by G. Lakoff (personal communication), in which verbs formerly supposed to be three-place Equi-governing predicates occurring in underlying structures like that schematized in·(13) instead represent two-place Raising-governing predicates as schematized in (i) or (ii), the standard Equi NP Deletion alternative schematized in (13) would not be a serious alternative. However, I will assume here that there is need to argue against (13) as an underlying structure for the constructions I am concerned with.

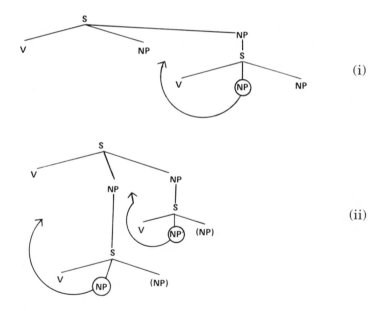

(i)

(ii)

[2]A similar argument for Raising using non-deictic *there* was first used by Rosenbaum; I believe that nonreferential *it* was first suggested as an argument by Postal, who attributes the idiom chunk argument to Perlmutter.

[3]John Lawler has noticed that this sentence, formed in a sincere attempt to communicate, with no malice aforethought, is a counterexample to Postal's claim that emphatic reflexives don't float into Equi'd complements.

[4]Some people won't like either sentence in (87) because of the generic *pictures of lizards*. Such facts will be discussed in Chapter IV.

III

Differences in the Object Status of Pre-*As* and Pre-*to* NP's

The surface structure object status of pre-*as* NP's is unchallenged, and virtually certain to remain so, while the object status of pre-*to* NP's in infinitive constructions has been challenged by Chomsky (1971). That is, grammarians agree that the major constituent break in the surface structure of sentences like (1) is before *as,* while they do not completely agree that the major break in sentences like (2) is before *to.*

(1) We regard him as being highly qualified for the job.
(2) We believe him to be highly qualified for the job.

The most reasonable alternative to a Raising analysis for sentences like (1) is an analysis in which the *as* clause is derived from an adverbial-like mystery source. I say this because of the evidence in Chapter II that sentences with *as* constructions, both putatively derived by Raising and not, do not show characteristics parallel to sentences usually analyzed as derived by Equi NP Deletion out of an object complement. For instance, if the missing subjects of *as* clauses are deleted by a rule, this rule does not demand the same type of coreference as regular Equi NP Deletion; and if there is difficulty in deciding whether a particular *as* construction is putatively Raising-derived or not, the rival analysis is an analysis in which the SVO string is an independent assertion, expanded on or qualified by the *as* clause.

The most reasonable alternative to a Raising analysis for sentences like (2), however, is an analysis in which the infinitive clause is derived from an underlying object complement; for although Bach (1974) quotes Staal as suggesting a source like that in (3) for the sentence in (4),

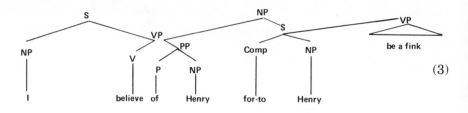

(3)

(4) I believe Henry to be a fink

No one has proposed, or is likely to propose, that such infinitives be derived from a mystery structure like (5):

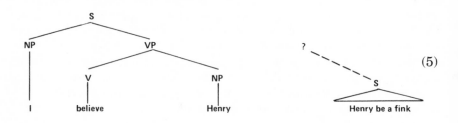

(5)

To summarize, then, there is complete agreement (or as complete agreement as is possible among linguists working in different theoretical frameworks) that all pre-*as* NP's are objects in surface structure, and that infinitives with proposition-embedding verbs (Postal's B-verbs) are derived from object complements. However, the origin of some pre-*as* NP's as subjects is controversial, as is the derived object status of some pre-*to* NP's.

In the previous chapter, I have argued that pairs like those in (1) and (7) are derived by Raising from object complements, and I am assuming that the major constituent break in the surface structure of such sentences is as marked.

(1) We regard him / as being highly qualified for the job.
(7) We consider him / to be highly qualified for the job.

In this chapter, however, I will argue that although such infinitives and *as* constructions have similar underlying structures, similar derivations, and similar surface structures, the total agreement among linguists about the surface structure object status of pre-*as* NP's and the lack of agreement about the object status of pre-*to* NP's is in a sense justified by a greater syntactic integrity of pre-*as* SVO strings than of pre-*to* SVO strings, and concomitantly more adverbial-like behavior of *as* clause adjuncts than infinitive clause adjuncts. In other words, raised objects in *as* constructions behave slightly more like objects than do raised objects in infinitive constructions, and the underlying subject origin of raised objects in *as* constructions is slightly more evident with regard to various phenomena than is the underlying subject origin of objects in pre-*as* position. I take this to be related to the fact that in *as* constructions not putatively derived by Raising, an *as* phrase or *as* clause clearly functions as an adverbial and a pre-*as* NP is always an object, while there exist infinitive clauses in which pre-*to* NP's clearly function as subjects. Examples (8–10) highlight the adverbial character of *as* in other constructions, and examples (11–13) show examples of non-Raising-derived infinitival clauses with their underlying subjects still functioning as subjects in surface structure.

(8)   As a child, I hated olives.
(9)   Marv described Susie as being nosy, but I wouldn't describe her that way.
(10) Mory was bumped off as a warning to others.
(11) Oh! For just one frog to come hopping by!
(12) For Jones to have done that is just incredible.
(13) What I'd really like is for you to shut up and listen.

What I am saying is that with respect to certain rules, objects in Raising-derived *as* constructions behave differently than objects in Raising-derived infinitive constructions, although such *as* constructions and infinitive constructions have the same underlying source and although both pre-*to* and pre-*as* NP's are in fact objects. Furthermore, I am saying that this difference in behavior is related to the fact that on the one hand, other superficially similar *as* + gerund clauses not derived by Raising are underlying adverbials, and the pre-*as* NP's in construction with them are objects in both underlying and surface structure, while on the other hand, pre-*to* NP's in other infinitive clauses not derived by Raising can function as subjects both in surface structure and in underlying structure. In other words, the behavior of an object NP and an adjunct in a construction derived by Raising is affected by the characteristics of object NP's in other constructions that are superficially similar but underlyingly different. A formal description of the facts would obviously call for transderivational rules of some sort, although I will not propose any such rules here.

I will now present evidence that in fact that is a slight difference in the object status of pre-*as* and pre-*to* NP's.

There are a number of rules that have the effect of isolating SVO strings. For most of these, it makes no easily discernible difference whether an SVO string is isolated from a Raising-derived *as* gerund adjunct or from a Raising-derived infinitival adjunct. For instance, the (a) and (b) sentences in (14) and (15) are probably equally bad.

(14a) *I don't want to regard Sue, but I do regard her, as being one of my enemies.

(14b) *I don't want to consider Sue, but I do consider her, to be one of my enemies.

(15a) *I didn't expect the inquiry to establish Fran, but they did establish her, as having left the party shortly before the accident.

(15b) *I didn't expect the lawyer to be able to prove Fran, but he did prove her, to have left the party shortly before the accident.

If there is any difference discernible between the (a) and (b) sentences above, I think the (b) sentences are slightly worse, but I find a great deal of difficulty in perceiving any difference at all. However, I do find a subtle difference in sentences in which Right Node Raising has isolated SVO strings before *as* clauses and infinitives.

(16a) Have the studies revealed pornography, or have they revealed drugs, as being the major cause of delinquency?

(16b) ?Have the studies revealed pornography, or have they revealed drugs, to be the major cause of delinquency?

(17a)   I regard you, and in fact you regard yourself, as being smarter than Harry.

(17b)   ?I consider you, and fact you consider yourself, to be smarter than Harry.

(18a)   ?We've established Gary, but we have yet to establish Ralph, as having been here before.

(18b)   *We've proven Gary, but we have yet to prove Ralph, to have been here before.

If others should detect differences in the (a) and (b) sentences in (14–18), I predict that the pre-*as* SVO strings will be judged as more isolable than the pre-*to* SVO strings (assuming an equal acceptance of such sentences without Right Node Raising).

Postal states that *alone*-final NP's, as in (19) and (20), occur only in subject position, and uses their non-occurrence in infinitival complements to support his position that pre-*to* NP's are not subjects but objects in surface structure.

(19)   Frank alone can cheer up Janet.

(20)   *Frank can cheer up Janet alone.

(21a)   Harry believes that Frank alone is able to cheer up Janet.

(21b)   *Harry believes Frank alone to be able to cheer up Janet.

I have marked the examples above as Postal predicts they should be marked, but in fact judgments about such sentences vary. Some people don't find (20) bad, and some people don't find (21b) bad; and these are not always the same people. For those who allow *alone*-final NP's in pre-infinitival object position, the quantifier *alone* often must be interpreted with narrow scope—that is, it can be interpreted as it would be if it were tacked on to the subject of a *that* clause. Examples are given below.

(22a)   Roger Mudd cheerfully reported C Troop alone to be crossing the border.

(22a = b) Roger Mudd cheerfully reported that C Troop alone was/is crossing the border.

(22a ≠ c) Other troops crossed the border, but Roger Mudd reported this only of C Troop.

(23a)   Their investigation has proved Frank alone to be equipped for such a job.

(23a = b) Their investigation has proved that Frank alone is equipped for such a job.

(23a ≠ c) Many people are equipped for such a job, but it is Frank alone that the investigation has been able to prove that about.

For people who allow *alone*-final NP's in pre-*as* object position, however, the quantifier *alone* can not be interpreted with narrow scope. For instance, if (24a) is acceptable, it means (24c) and not (24b).

(24a)   Roger Mudd reported C Troop alone as crossing the border.

(24a ≠ b) Roger Mudd reported that C Troop alone was/is crossing the border.

(24a = c) Other troops may have crossed the border, but Roger Mudd reported this of C Troop only.

(25a)   Our investigation has established Frank alone as having been in the basement at the time of the fire.

(25a ≠ b) Our investigation has established that Frank alone was in the basement at the time of the fire.

(25a = c) Other people may have been in the basement at the time of the fire, but we've been able to establish this of Frank only.

Other quantifiers can be used with the same patterning of results, but before I examine them, I would like to discuss an argument of Postal's that is similar to his *alone*-final argument but that is more reliable across variation.

Postal observes that *not*-initial NP's like those in (26) and (27) below do not occur in non-subject position.

(26)   [Postal's 25]
(26a)   Not many gorillas have learned to tap dance.
(26b)   Not much sense can be made out of that proposal.
(26c)   Not many Turks speak Yiddish.
(26d)   Not many Albanians have been interviewed by Sevareid.
(26e)   Not many farmers are easy to convince.
(27)   [Postal's 26]
(27a)   *Joe kissed not many models.
(27b)   *Jane earns not much money.
(27c)   *Jane talked to Bob about not many problems.
(27d)   *I bought Kangaroos from not many Australians.

The exact nature of this constraint is discussed in more detail in Postal (1974), but the generalization stated above stands, and as far as I know, it stands more firmly for a greater number of speakers than does his similar generalization about *alone*-final NP's. I bring it up here because I have found some cases in which *not*-initial NP's don't sound very bad with infinitives, although *not*-initial NP's are consistently very bad with *as* clauses. The sentences below are examples.

(28a) ? This latest communique proves not much to be happening at the home office.

(28b) ? It's true that the polls have shown not many people to be in favor of the President's staying in office, (but I think that most people would prefer that he resign rather than be impeached).

(28c) ? The Evening News reports not many people to be pleased with the upcoming tax increase.

(29a) * Our intelligence has established not much as happening at their home office.

(29b) * It's true that the polls have revealed not many people as being in favor of the President's staying in office, (but I think that most people would prefer that he resign rather than be impeached).

(29c) * The Evening News reports not many people as being pleased with the upcoming tax increase.

It should be noted here that the relative acceptability judgments shown above are related to relative strictness of constraints on what kind of constituent can be raised to object position. For instance, non-referring NP's and indefinites do not occur freely in object position with infinitives and occur only rarely in pre-*as* object position; thus, the relative pattern of acceptability in (28) and (29) is echoed in (30) and (31).

(30a) This latest communique proves a lot to be happening in the home office.

(30b) It's true that the polls have shown most people to be in favor of the President's staying in office.

(30c) The Evening News reports many people to be pleased with the upcoming tax increase.

(31a) * Our intelligence has established a lot as happening in their home office.

(31b) ? It's true that the polls have revealed most people as being in favor of the President's staying in office.

(31c) * The Evening News reports many people as being pleased with the upcoming tax increase.

Although I have left the sentences in (30) unmarked, some speakers find these questionable also, although not as bad as the sentences in (31).

These facts, in turn, are related to the broader question of the scope of quantifiers in pre-*as* and in pre-*to* position. Although the correct principles involved in interpretation of quantifier scope are hidden from me, I will assume here, following Postal, and Ioup 1974, that such principles at least involve surface structure clause membership and grammatical function. With regard to the two constructions under discussion, there is a consistently greater possibility for a quantifier in pre-*to* derived object position to have narrow scope, that is, a scope that includes only the complement. However, quantifiers in pre-*as* position will have only wide scope. I offer this as more evidence that NP's raised with infinitives can still function to some extent as subjects of the infinitive complement, while NP's raised with *as* constructions cannot.

It is practically impossible to present variation-free evidence both with regard to quantifier scope and with regard to Raising to Object Position. The problem is further complicated by the fact that the nature of the main verb influences whether a quantifier in derived object position is interpreted with wide or narrow scope. For instance, I tend to interpret (32a) with wide scope, thus not equal to 32b); but (33a), with a stative sense of *prove,* is more compatible with a narrow scope reading.

(32a)   John proved someone in the room to be lying.
(32a $\neq$ b) John proved that someone in the room was lying.
(33a)   This evidence proves someone in the room to be lying.
(33a = b) This evidence proves that someone in the room is lying.

A still further complication is the tendency for some quantifiers to be interpreted with a wider or more narrow scope than others. A hierarchy of quantifier scope is mentioned and attributed to Leben in G. Lakoff (1973), and is further examined by Ioup (1974), who observes that the larger the set specified by a particular quantifier, the greater will be the tendency for the quantifier to be interpreted with wide scope.

Among all this variation and complexity, however, I think that some generalizations pertinent to the topic under discussion can be salvaged. For although a narrow scope reading is possible for at least some speakers for quantifiers in pre-*to* object position, I know of no speakers who will agree to a narrow-scope reading of quantifiers in pre-*as* object position. The examples that follow in (34–36) are unmarked as to acceptability, although the sentences with *as*, particularly, will be questionable for a number of speakers.

(34a) The evidence in this folder proves every witness to be lying.
(34b) The evidence in this folder proves most of the witnesses to
       be lying.
(34c) The evidence in this folder proves some of the witnesses to
       be lying.
(34d) The evidence in this folder proves a few of the witnesses to
       be lying.

I can get a narrow-scope reading, that is, a reading parallel to those
in (35), on all of the sentences in (34).

(35)   The evidence in this folder proves that
       $\left\{ \begin{array}{l} \text{every witness is} \\ \text{most of the witnesses are} \\ \text{some of the witnesses are} \\ \text{a few of the witnesses are} \end{array} \right\}$
       lying.

The Leben/Ioup hierarchy predicts (correctly, I think) that a narrow-
scope reading will be hardest for (a) and easiest for (d) in (34) above.
Presumably, the same scale of difference applies to the sentences in
(36), but I find it impossible to get a narrow-scope reading for any of
the sentences in (36).

(36a) The evidence in this folder establishes every witness as hav-
       ing lied.
(36b) The evidence in this folder establishes most of the witnesses
       as having lied.
(36c) The evidence in this folder establishes some of the witnesses
       as having lied.
(36d) The evidence in this folder establishes a few of the witnesses
       as having lied.

Even though the ultimate importance of this data rests on an understanding of the principles determining quantifier scope, I think that
it shows a vestige of the former subjecthood of the raised NP in infinitive constructions that is not shared by an NP in an analogous position in *as* constructions.

Postal suggests the following principle to constrain the placement
of "sentential adverbs", or adverbs whose scope of modification is not
less than the main clause.

(37) [Postal's 137] A sentential adverb can*not* be inserted in a complement clause.

Two of his examples follow:

(38)   [Postal's 136]
(38a) I can prove that Bob easily outweighed Martha's goat.
(38b) I can prove Bob easily to have outweighed Martha's goat.

Postal's main interest in (38a) and (38b) was in the fact that in (38a), *easily* must modify only the complement or part of the complement, while in (38b) it can be construed as modifying the main clause. However, in discussing (38b), he claims that *easily* can also be construed as modifying the complement, and he makes a similar claim for recently in (39b).

(39)   [Postal's 133]
(39a) I have found that Bob recently has been morose.
(39b) I have found Bob recently to be morose.

My own judgments aren't very clear about sentences with infinitives like those in (38b) and (39b), but I do think that it is never possible in *as* constructions for an adverb after an object derived by Raising to be ambiguously construed as modifying either the main clause or just the complement. Always, I think, such an adverb must be construed as modifying the main clause. The sentences in (40b) and (41b) contrast with (38b) and (39b) in this regard.

(40a) We can establish that Bob easily outweighed Martha's goat on a number of occasions.
(40b) We can establish Bob easily as having outweighed Martha's goat on a number of occasions.
(41a) Sam regards Bob as only occasionally being morose enough to worry about.
(41b) Sam regards Bob only occasionally as being morose enough to worry about.

While in (38) and (39), *easily* and *recently* with infinitives may be construed ambiguously, this is not true for *easily* and *occasionally* with *as* constructions in (40) and (41), which can only be construed as modifying the main clause. The constituent break before *to* that allows the placement of adverbs modifying either the main clause or the complement clause apparently differs from the constituent break before *as,* which accommodates only adverbs with higher scope. There are many ways to phrase this fact, according to particular theories of adverb placement and interpretation of adverb scope, but I think that it is clear that this is another way in which an infinitival construction derived by Raising still functions more like a whole object complement with a subject than does an *as* construction derived by Raising.

Postal observes that in general, backward application of Equi NP Deletion occurs only when the pronoun to be deleted is commanded by its antecedent in surface structure, as in his examples (78a) and (b) and (79a) and (b), repeated here in (42) and (43).

(42a)   Shooting himself$_i$ amused Tony$_i$.
(42b)   Losing his$_i$ wallet annoyed Max$_i$.
(43a) * Shooting himself$_i$ amused Barbara because Tony$_i$ was unpleasant.
(43b) * Criticizing himself$_i$ annoyed the girl who loved Tony$_i$.

The relative acceptability of infinitives with Backwards Equi is used by Postal as one argument for Raising, since only in a Raising analysis is the deleted pronoun in (44b) (his [81b]) commanded by the controller *Bob*.

(44a) * Criticizing himself$_i$ proved (that) Bob$_i$ was humble.
(44b) ? Criticizing himself$_i$ proved Bob$_i$ to be humble.

The judgments on the sentences above are meant to be relative judgments. Some people reject both (44a) and (b), and although Postal claims that nobody will accept (44a), I have found that some people do. However, I believe that the relative judgments of (44a) and (b) will be consistent. I also believe that (45) will be consistently judged as better than (44b), for those people who accept (46) (and not everyone does):

(45)   Criticizing himself$_i$ immediately established Bob$_i$ as being humble.
(46)   His$_i$ criticizing himself$_i$ immediately established Bob$_i$ as being humble.

The markings on the sentences in (47) reflect the pattern of acceptability I predict, although individual judgment will vary and it must be recognized that not everyone will accept (48).

(47a)   Playing with himself$_i$ like that established Bob$_i$ as being indifferent to public reaction.

(47b) ? Playing with himself$_i$ like that showed Bob$_i$ to be indiffer-
       ent to public reaction.

(47c) * Playing with himself$_i$ like that proved that Bob$_i$ was/is in-
       different to public reaction.

(48)   His$_i$ playing with himself$_i$ like that established Bob$_i$ as
       being indifferent to public reaction.

Backward Equi, then, provides other evidence that the object status
pre *as* NP's is more secure than the object status of pre *to* NP's.

In the previous pages I have shown that with regard to several
phenomena assumed to be sensitive to clausal boundaries, raised pre-
infinitival object NP's behave slightly more like subject NP's of object
complements than do raised NP's that are in *as* constructions. I have
taken this to be related to the historical fact that no one has ever
challenged the object status of pre-*as* NP's, while the object status of
pre-*to* NP's has been questioned. I will also take it to be related to the
fact that the constraints on Raising-derived *as* constructions and infinitival constructions discussed in the next chapter are similar but
more stringent for *as* constructions.

As for a formalization of the facts discussed in this chapter, there
is in present theory no formally defined concept of "partial direct object"
or "vestigial subject," although the globally defined notion of cyclic
subject has been used when the notion of "subject at the time of application of a particular rule" has been shown to be insufficient to
specify the operation of certain rules, such as number agreement (Andrews, 1971; G. Lakoff, 1970) and extraction from complex nominals
(Postal, 1974). G. Lakoff (personal communication) suggests that difference in object status of pre-*as* and pre-*to* NP's can be reflected in a
grammar such as that discussed in G. Lakoff (1973), in which rules
like Raising have the status of well-formedness conditions on adjacent
pairs of trees in a derivation. In such a grammar, which Lakoff calls
a *correspondence grammar,* rules can specify a degree of well-formedness between two trees, global rules than specifying a degree of well-
formedness between two or more non-adjacent trees in a derivation.
With regard to the two constructions derived by Raising to object position, then, the degree of well-formedness of a derivation in which a
node is in subject position of an object complement in one tree and has
a corresponding node in object position of the matrix clause in an
adjacent tree—that is, the degree of well-formedness of a derivation
with regard to Raising to object position—would be greater for sentences with *as* constructions than for sentences with infinitives. This
might correspond to a transformational grammar in which Raising to
Object Position applies only to a degree with infinitives, although of

course no such revision of transformational grammar has been proposed.

Degrees of objecthood and subjecthood are related, I think, to the concept of clausiness as explored in recent work by Ross (cf. Ross, 1972b and 1973b). In the cases discussed in this chapter, for example, the partial subjecthood of pre-*to* NP's as opposed to pre-*as* NP's is related to a greater degree of clausiness of infinitive constructions as compared to gerunds in general and *as*-gerunds in particular. That is, both pre-*to* NP's and pre-*as* NP's can bear residual, partial grammatical relations to the clause they originate in, while at the same time bearing a strong but not complete object relation to a higher clause, and the varying degrees of strength of grammatical relationships are directly related to how "clausy" is the surface structure realization of an underlying object complement.

The phenomena discussed in this chapter crucially involve the notion of membership in a higher or lower clause, and subtly distinguish between pre-*to* NP's and pre-*as* NP's. Many other phenomena do not distinguish between NP's in these two positions; in other words, although these phenomena may also be sensitive to membership in a particular clause, the strength of objecthood or subjecthood that they require is possessed by both pre-*to* and pre-*as* NP's. It may also be the case that the phenomena Postal used in *On Raising* to show the object status of pre-*to* NPs test different aspects of subjecthood or objecthood, among them the clausiness of the surface structure realization of the complement, the semantic cohesiveness of the derived SVO string, and the strength of the major constituent break; and that the rules discussed in this chapter crucially involve a particular aspect of the construct "object."

A theory with squishes and global rules could undoubtedly handle the facts described here, but of course the crucial question is what the *right* way of handling the facts is. How to express formally such notions as "functions less as a surface structure object", "functions more as subject of a complement," "functions more/less as an independent clause" is a less crucial problem than why such differences exist and what other phenomena they are related to. In the next two chapters I examine some semantic and pragmatic characteristics of *as* constructions, infinitive constructions and related constructions, in an effort to explore these more basic questions.

IV

Constraints on Raising

INTRODUCTION

Many Raising verbs that occur with infinitive constructions also occur with *that* clauses as object complements in surface structure. However, the formation of *that* clauses is much less constrained than the formation of infinitives by Raising; it is by no means true that one can form an acceptable sentence with an infinitive clause parallel to every acceptable sentence with an object *that* clause. In this chapter, I will examine what I consider to be semantic and pragmatic constraints on Raising to pre-infinitival object position and on Raising to pre-*as* clause object position, in an effort to discover semantic and pragmatic correlates of the syntactic process of merging two separate underlying clauses into a surface structure $S \ V \ O + Adjunct$ string. I will show that the constraints on Raising are similar for *as* constructions and infinitives, and that the stronger derived object status of pre-*as* NP's, discussed in the previous chapter, accompanies an increased strictness of these constraints.

CONSTRAINTS ON WHAT CAN BE RAISED

In a paper presented at the 1973 Winter Linguistics Society of America meetings, Akmajian observed that while prepositional phrases can sometimes serve as subjects of sentences, as in (1), and can be raised to subject position, as in (2), they cannot be raised to object position, as in (3). The examples in (1–3) are Akmajian's, as are the judgments as marked.

> (1)   From London to Paris is a long way.
> (2)   From London to Paris seems to be a long way.
> (3)   * In those days, they believed from London to Paris to be a long way.

Akmajian's paper contains a number of keen observations about differences in Raising to subject position and Raising to object position. He suggests that Raising to subject position must be stated in terms of some general, perhaps extended notion of "subject," rather than in terms of any categorical notion such as NP. The data in his paper suggest that Raising to object position, on the other hand, can be stated in terms of the categorical label NP.

Although for Akmajian,[1] and others, a constituent raised to object position must belong to the syntactic category NP, this is not true for all speakers. Some speakers will accept (3), for instance, while some are even more conservative than Akmajian and will be doubtful about (2). It has been my experience, however, that speakers will generally agree that (4) and (5) are better than (2) and (3), respectively.

> (4)   From Aix to Nice seems to be the most grueling part of the race.
> (5)   In those days, they believed from Aix to Nice to be the most grueling part of the race.

The reason, I think, is that in (6),

> (6)   From Aix to Nice is the most grueling part of the race.

the prepositional phrase *from Aix to Nice* refers to a stretch of land viewed not as an abstraction but as perceivable through one's senses. In (1), however, the prepositional phrase *from London to Paris* refers not to a stretch of land that can be recalled in images, but to a distance that is to be calculated rather than experienced. For want of better terminology, I will label as reification vs. abstraction, the distinction I am trying to make between viewing something as a perceivable object vs. viewing something as abstract and not directly experienceable. Since not everybody accepts *believe* as a Raising verb, I offer (7a) and (7b) as clearer examples of the differences I am trying to put into relief.

(7a) ? South Africans consider from Capetown to Hannasville to be a long way.

(better:)

(7b) Bike racers consider from Capetown to Hannasville to be the easiest stretch in the race.

The reification vs. abstraction distinction also works for some people with regard to time expressions. In (8), *after 4:00* refers to a point in time viewed as an abstract measurement, while in (9), *around 4:00* refers to an experienceable stretch in time.

(8) After 4:00 is the earliest they'll allow me to read my mail.
(9) Around 4:00 is the most dismal part of the day for elderly shut-ins.

If there is a difference perceivable, (11), in which the raised constituent refers to an experienceable stretch of time, will be perceived as better than (10).

(10) Max reports after 4:00 to be the earliest they'll allow him to read his mail.
(11) Max reports around 4:00 to be the most dismal part of the day for him in his new surroundings.

For some speakers, then, prepositional phrases can be raised to object position if they refer not to an abstract measurement but to a stretch of land or time viewed as experiencable through one's senses.

Although for speakers like Akmajian, the raised constituent's belonging to the category NP is a necessary condition for Raising to object position, as far as I know, it is not a sufficient condition for any speakers. Not just any NP can be felicitously raised to object position, and the restrictions on what kind of NP may be raised are often reminiscent of restrictions on what kind of prepositional phrase can be raised (for those speakers who allow raising of preopositional phrases). That is, these restrictions seem to all be in some way related to the referring nature of the NP involved. For instance, Raising to object position lifts referring subject NP's like *Sam* in (12) more easily than attributively referring definite descriptions like *Jim's murderer* in (13).

(12) Sam is Jim's murderer.
(13) Jim's murderer is Sam.

(14) and (15) contain examples of NP's containing definite descriptions that resist Raising.

(14a)   The lawyers proved Sam to be Fred's assailant.
(14b)   The lawyers proved Fred's assailant to be Sam.
(15a)   I consider Rossini to be the villain.
(15b)   ?I consider the villain to be Rossini.

This is only a tendency and not a hard-and-fast rule, however; some speakers will accept the (b) sentences in (14) and (15), and I have so far found no one who would question (16b).

(16a)   Most people believe Rossini to be the villain.
(16b)   Most people believe the villain to be Rossini.

I know of no cases where a verb allows Raising of a non-referring descriptive NP but does not allow Raising of a referring NP, however.[2]

Generic noun phrases sometimes resist Raising. I take this to be related to the previously discussed tendency for Raising to lift only those non-NP's that refer to objects experienced in the physical world and not to lift non-referring NP's used as attributive definite descriptions; that is, I assume that a noun phrase that refers to a class of entities rather than to a particular entity is in some (admittedly unclear) sense definitely referring.

Variation is particularly wide with regard to what kinds of generics resist Raising with what kind of verbs. Generics with definite articles are raised just as easily as non-generics, as far as I can tell, and most (but not all) people will accept Raising of plural generics with no article, as in (17c).

(17a)   The tests revealed Frank to be a lot less intelligent than the typical chess player.

(17b) The tests revealed the typical teenager to be a lot less knowledgeable about drugs than was expected.

(17c) The tests revealed teenagers to be a lot less knowledgeable about drugs than was expected.

Other generics do resist Raising, however, although people vary in their reactions considerably.

(18a) ? The tests revealed a typical teenager to be a lot less knowledgeable about drugs than one might expect.

(18b) ? The tests revealed a teenager with any smarts at all to be a lot more knowledgeable about drugs than the average policeman.

(18c) * The tests revealed any teenager to be a lot more knowledgeable about drugs than most 45 year olds.

(19)   I believe
$\left\{ \begin{array}{l} \text{the typical beaver} \\ (?)\,\text{a beaver} \\ ?*\,\text{a beaver with any brains at all} \\ *\,\text{any beaver} \end{array} \right\}$
to be a lot smarter than any domestic pet.

Not only does this constraint vary across speakers and for different generics, but the nature of the verb governing Raising influences acceptability judgments. The judgments in (20) are my own.

(20a) (?)We believe a suburbanite with any pretensions at all to be acutely aware of how much his neighbor is spending.

(20b) ?This proves a suburbanite with any pretensions at all to be acutely aware of how much his neighbor is spending.

(20c) ?*The evidence confirms a suburbanite with any pretensions at all to be acutely aware of how much his neighbor is spending.

(21a) They consider an accountant with any brains at all to be capable of making it in the big city.

(21b) (?)I believe an accountant with any brains at all to be capable of making it in the big city.

(21c) ?Our study confirms an accountant with any brains at all to be capable of making it in the big city.

I do not know how to interpret this variation, but I contend that the resistance of some generics to Raising is related to the fact that generics do not definitely refer to a single entity. The fact that generics with definite articles like *the typical beaver, the average American,* etc. do not resist Raising is evidence that I have not captured the constraint correctly, but the fact that a definite article is used with these generics seems to support the idea that something like definiteness of reference, or whatever it is that determines when a definite article is appropriate, is involved.

I am not sure how to refer to the noun phrase *the littlest thing,* in sentences like (22).

(22) The littlest thing throws him into a tizzy.

Fauconnier (1974) argues that superlatives like the *most insignificant detail* and *the slightest show of affection* in (23) and (24) are related to the quantifier *any,* as in the paraphrases in (25) and (26).

(23) The most insignificant detail throws him into a tizzy.
(24) Mary disapproves of the slightest show of affection.
(25) Any detail, even the most insignificant, throws him into a tizzy.
(26) Mary disapproves of any show of affection, even the slightest.

The littlest thing, then, is probably related to *anything,* although (27) is a very odd paraphrase of (22).

(27) ? Anything, even the littlest, throws him into a tizzy.

In any case, however *the littlest thing* is to be analyzed, it is clearly not referring, and it resists Raising.

(28a) We believe your strange behavior to be irritating to him.
(28b) * We believe the littlest thing to be irritating to him.
(29a) I acknowledge Tricia to be annoying to sensitive people like you and me, but. . .
(29b) * I acknowledge the littlest thing to be annoying to sensitive people like you and me, but. . .

Raising of superlatives whose nouns have more semantic content than does *thing* is slightly better, as in (30) and (31).

(30) ? We believe the slightest discrepancy to be irritating to him.
(31) ? I acknowledge the slightest off-note to be annoying to sensitive people like you and me, but. . .

John Lawler points out that all these sentences are better, for some reason, when *even* occurs with the superlatives.

(32) We believe even the littlest thing to be annoying to him.
(33) ? I acknowledge even the littlest thing to be annoying to sensitive people like you and me.
(34) We believe even the slightest discrepancy to be irritating to him.
(35) I acknowledge even the slightest off-note to be annoying to sensitive people like you and me.

Another peculiarity is that the resistance of superlatives to Raising only holds with proposition-embedding verbs like *believe, acknowledge, prove,* etc.; (36) and (37) with *allow* and *want* seem perfectly acceptable.

(36) They allow the littlest thing to annoy them.
(37) I want the slightest infraction to be brought to my attention.

Nonreferential indefinite NP's also resist Raising to object position, although like the facts for generics, the facts about nonreferential indefinites vary with the matrix verb and the particular indefinite, as well as varying idiolectally. Partee (1971b) gives the sentence in (38), for example, in which *a Communist* need not be referential.

(38) John believes a Communist to have been at the heart of the plot.

That is, in (38), John may believe that the person who was at the heart of the plot was a Communist, without either John or the speaker knowing who that person was. In my judgment, the indefinite *some Communist* in (39) may marginally be non-referring, that is, interpreted as parallel to *some Communist* in (40),

(39) John believes some Communist to have been at the heart of the plot.
(40) John believes that some Communist was at the heart of the plot, but neither John nor I can figure out who it was.

and *somebody* in (41) may likewise be (marginally) non-referring.

(41) John believes somebody to have been waiting to ambush him.

Quantification with the nonreferring *some* (sm) is worse for me in (42), however, although others will accept it.

> (42) ?John believes sm Communists to have been at the heart of the plot.

With *prove* and *confirm,* the facts seem to be clearer. I have found that most people will agree with my hesitation at at least the e variants in (43) and (44).

> (43a)   ?John proved an outsider to be agitating for removal of the Chairman.
> (43b)   ?John proved somebody to be agitating for removal of the Chairman (but neither John nor I know who it is).
> (43c)   ?John proved some outsider to be agitating for removal of the Chairman (but neither John nor I know who it is).
> (43d) ?*John proved sm outsiders to be agitating for removal of the Chairman.
> (43e)   *John proved sm people to be agitating for removal of the Chairman.
> (44a)   ?The investigation confirmed an employee to be stealing from the slush fund.
> (44b) (?)The investigation confirmed somebody to be stealing from the slush fund (but we don't know who it is yet).
> (44c)   ?The investigation confirmed some employee to be stealing from the slush fund (but we don't know who it is yet).
> (44d) ?*The investigation confirmed sm employees to be stealing from the slush fund.
> (44e)   *The investigation confirmed sm people to be stealing from the slush fund.

Quine (1960) claims that in the example repeated below in (45), *Cicero* is in purely referential position.

> (45) Tom believes Cicero to have denounced Catiline.

That is, Quine claims that, while the sentence given here as (46) is false if Tom knows that someone named Tully denounced Catiline but doesn't know that *Tully* and *Cicero* are different names for the same person, this is not true for (45).

> (46) Tom believes that Cicero denounced Catiline.

That is, under the circumstances described, in which Tom is not aware that Tully and Cicero were the same person, (46) is false although (47) is true.

(47) Tom believes that Tully denounced Catiline.

Quine claims that under the same circumstances, however, (45) is true, that is, that the sentence in (45) does not allow opacity of reference.

I agree with Partee (1971b) that the facts aren't clear for (45). With regard to Raising verbs generally, though, I think that Quine's intuition is right, in that it is more difficult to get an opaque reading for subjects of *that* clauses.

The facts are slightly clearer for verbs that describe actions involving speech acts. The act of proving the truth of a proposition usually involves speaking or writing, for instance; and *that* clauses as objects of *prove* have a feeling of quotation that a clause broken up by Raising lacks. I think it is more difficult to get an opaque reading for (48a) than for (48b);

(48a) Last night, Dr. Pierce flamboyantly proved Clark Kent to be suffering from an Asian blood disease.
(48b) Last night, Dr. Pierce flamboyantly proved that Clark Kent was/is suffering from an Asian blood disease.

With verbs that more directly describe speech acts, that clauses contain fairly direct quotations, and references therein are strongly opaque. Raising with these verbs makes it almost impossible to get an opaque reading for the raised NP. For instance, (50a) might be used in a conversation about Superman by someone observing a series of events who knows that Clark Kent is Superman and that his addressee knows it too, but I don't think that (50b) could be used in such a situation if the judges knew only that Clark Kent had entered and won the race.

(50a) The judges have proved Superman to be the winner of the gunnysack race.
(50b) The judges have proved that Superman is the winner of the gunnysack race.

I find the facts quite clear, here, but one informant, Sandra Browne, has told me that she considers even (50b) appropriate under the circumstances as described.

It seems, then, that there is a tendency for Raising to lift constituents that definitely refer, although this is by no means a strict either-or principle, applying to a rigorously defined concept of reference. The examples given above have all included infinitive constructions, but *as* constructions derived by Raising are constrained similarly. For *as* constructions, however, the constraints are consistently stricter.

When I first studied *as* constructions, it appeared to me that Raising does not lift prepositional phrases into pre-*as* object position, no matter what they refer to, as seems to be indicated by (51) and (52).

(51) * In those days, they regarded from Aix to Nice as being the most grueling part of the race.

(52) ? Research has established around 4:00 as being the most dismal time of day for elderly shut-ins.

With my constant exposure to all kinds of Raising sentences, however, I find (53) not very bad at all; and others have told me that they find it "almost good."

(53) ? Somehow I pictured from Aix to Nice as being more hilly than it actually is.

Notice that the verb *picture* forces a non-abstract interpretation of *from Aix to Nice,* as well as a less abstract interpretation of time phrases.

(54) * For some reason I pictured after 4:00 as being the earliest they'll allow me to read my mail.

(55) ? For some reason I pictured around 4:00 as being the most dismal time of day around here.

George Lakoff has offered (56) and (57) as good sentences, and I agree with his judgments.

(56) I have always regarded after lunch as being the nicest time of day.

(57) I have always regarded under the bed as being the best place to screw.

However, a change of verb, as in (58) and (59), affects the acceptability of these sentences.

(58) ? Scientists have determined after lunch as being the best time of day for hemophiliacs.

(59) * Masters and Johnson have established under the bed as being the best place to screw.

Non-referring definite descriptions do not readily occur as derived objects before *as*.

(60a)   Mary simply refuses to acknowledge Charles as being the one responsible for the situation.

(60b)   *Mary simply refuses to acknowledge the one responsible for the situation as being Charles.

(61a)   I regard Rossini as being the real villain.

(61b)   *I regard the real villain as being Rossini.

However, those who accept (14b), which I repeat here with my own judgment marked, may also accept (62).

(14b)   ?The lawyers proved Fred's assailant to be Sam.

(62)   ?The lawyers established Fred's assailant as being Sam.

Raising-derived *as* constructions allow generics somewhat less freely than do infinitive constructions.

(63)   I regard
$$\left\{ \begin{array}{l} \text{the typical beaver} \\ \text{?a beaver} \\ \text{?*a beaver with any brains at all} \\ \text{*any beaver} \end{array} \right\}$$
as being a lot smarter than any household animal.

(64a)   *Research has established an accountant with any ambition at all as being capable of making it in the big city.

(64b)   *This reveals an accountant with any ambition at all as being capable of making it in the big city.

(64c)   *Our economist recognizes an accountant with any ambition at all as being capable of making it in the big city.

Similarly, non-referring superlatives are even more strange with *as* constructions than with infinitives.

(65)   *I recognize the slightest off note as being annoying to sensitive people like you and me.

(66)   *We regard the littlest thing as being upsetting to him.

John Lawler points out that even the presence of *even* won't save these examples.

(67)   *I recognize even the slightest off note as being annoying
       to sensitive people like you and me.
(68)   *We regard even the littlest thing as being upsetting to him.

With a strong raising verb like *regard* and a superlative with a noun
phrase that has more semantic content than does *thing*, however, other
examples are good. The following examples were suggested to me by
George Lakoff:

(69) Nixon regards the slightest criticism as being tantamount to
      treason.
(70) The Church regards the humblest peasant as being worthy
      of redemption.

Non-referential indefinite NP's are not good in pre-*as* object position, which follows from the fact noted in Chapter III, that quantifiers
in pre-*as* position have wide scope only.

(71) * We've established

$$\begin{Bmatrix} \text{an outsider} \\ \text{somebody} \\ \text{some outsider} \\ \text{sm outsiders} \\ \text{sm people} \end{Bmatrix}$$

       as agitating for removal of the Chairman (but we don't
       know who $\begin{Bmatrix} \text{they are} \\ \text{it is} \end{Bmatrix}$).

The facts about opacity are the same for *as* constructions as they
are for infinitives, as far as I can tell. For instance, I find that only
(72a) is appropriate if Superman in the persona of Clark Kent has
entered and won the race, even if the conversation is about Superman
and is being carried on by people who are of Clark Kent's true identity.

(72a) The judges have announced Superman as the winner of the
       gunnysack race.
(72b) The judges have announced that Superman is the winner
       of the gunnysack race.

It is true for both *as* constructions and infinitives, then, that Raising tends to lift constituents that definitely refer, and this tendency
is stronger for *as* constructions than for infinitives. The facts indicating
this tendency are summarized in the table in (73).

(73)

**CONSTRAINTS ON WHAT KIND OF CONSTITUENT
CAN BE RAISED TO OBJECT POSITION**

Constituent	Pre-to Position	Pre-as Position	Differences in the Two Positions
a. prepositional phrases	For some speakers, can be raised if "reified"	Almost never raisable	Pre-*as* position more restricted
b. non-referring definite descriptions	Limited Raising for some speakers	Possibly never raised	Pre-*as* position more restricted
c. generics	Limited Raising	More severely limited Raising	Pre-*as* position more restricted
d. superlatives	Limited Raising	Severely limited Raising	Pre-*as* position more restricted
e. indefinite, specific NP's	Limited Raising	No Raising	Pre-*as* position more restricted
f. opacity	Opaque reading more difficult than for non-Raised NP's	Opaque reading more difficult than for non-Raised NP's	No difference

Since the facts about definite reference described in this chapter are another aspect of facts about the scope of quantification discussed in the previous chapter, it is not clear whether the quantification facts actually belong in a chapter about constraints on Raising, or whether the facts about definite reference actually belong in a chapter about differences in the object status of pre-*as* and pre-*to* NP's. Rather than talk about constraints on Raising, perhaps I should use the theoretically more neutral phrase "characteristics of constructions derived by Raising," since I have not committed myself to a particular way of formalizing the generalizations I have noticed. In any case, it is quite clear that the facts about Raising noticed in this chapter are closely related to the surface structure consequences of Raising, and that the relative strictness of pre-*as* object position with regard to non-referential NP's like weather and time *it*, non-deictic *there*, as well as the non-referential NP's discussed in this chapter, is related to the relatively stronger integrity of SVO strings before *as* constructions.

CONSTRAINTS ON COMPLEMENTS
BROKEN UP BY RAISING

Introduction

In the previous section, I discussed special characteristics of raised constituents in contrast to the unrestricted nature of non-raised subjects of *that* clauses. In this section, I will examine special characteristics of complements broken up by Raising, in contrast to the unrestricted character of complements that surface in *that* clauses. Again, it will be seen that the constraints on what kind of complement can be broken up by Raising are similar for *as* constructions and infinitives, and that if there are differences in strictness of such constraints, *as* constructions will be formed less freely than infinitive constructions.

Speaker Viewing Differences

I would like to point out a distinction relevant to the topic at hand, between propositions that are viewed as being about matters of human judgment and those that are viewed as being about empirically verifiable matters of fact. For example, the statement "Harry is an immoral person" concerns a matter of judgment; the term "immoral" is meaningless apart from social norms, which obviously vary. A statement like "Harry was born on a Friday," on the other hand, is viewed as being true or false quite independently of human values or judgments. Of course, practically any given proposition can in a suitable context be viewed as a matter of fact or a matter of judgment. For instance, although out of context the proposition "this hammock is comfortable" would probably be interpreted as expressing someone's personal judgment about how the hammock suits him, it could also be used to express the finding of a study in which standards of comfort have been defined and different hammocks have been tested against this standard. And even a proposition involving an event, such as "Harry made some egg rolls last night," could be viewed as a matter of judgment if what is in question is what it is appropriate to call the things that Harry made.

The distinction I am drawing is virtually the same as that labeled *objective* vs. *subjective* in Bolinger (1973). Bolinger observed that explicit performatives, epistemic modals and degree words are related in that they all show the speaker's awareness that the truth of a proposition is not absolute but depends on one's view of things, and he uses the following test to bring into relief the objective-subjective difference: When the content of an assertion is viewed as being "in the nature of things, above and beyond the assertion", it can't be followed by expressions like *to have impressed that audience, to have annoyed them, for them to have tolerated it,* etc. The examples in (74) and (75) are Bolinger's.

(74a) ? Harry is Mexican, to have made such frijoles.
(74b) Harry is incompetent, to have made such frijoles.
(75a) ? His music was symphonic to have impressed that audience.
(75b) His music was brilliant to have impressed that audience.

The relevance to constraints on Raising of the *matters of judgment* vs. *matters of fact* distinction is this: Raising breaks up complements viewed as matters of judgment more readily than it breaks up complements viewed as matters of fact. One instance of this has already been given by Bolinger (1967b), who says that in his speech, *believe* is more likely to occur with infinitives in a sense close to that of *consider*, as in (76a), than in a conjectural sense close to *understand*, as in (76b).

(76a) I $\begin{Bmatrix} \text{consider} \\ \text{believe} \end{Bmatrix}$ John to be a suitable candidate

(76b) I $\begin{Bmatrix} \text{understand} \\ \text{?believe} \end{Bmatrix}$ John to be a French teacher.

Obviously, since *understand* is a Raising verb in (69b), there is no across-the-board stricture against Raising breaking up complements viewed as matters of fact. Still, the generalization holds true in other cases, such as, for example, with *find*. With *find,* as with *believe,* objectively viewed propositions about empirically verifiable, either-or matters of fact are most appropriate in *that* clauses, but when *find* is used to describe someone's personal experience or judgment, an infinitive is more appropriate.

(77a)   When I looked in the files, I found that she was Mexican.
(77b)   ?When I looked in the files, I found her to be Mexican.
(78a)   ?I find that Harry is amusing, although everyone else thinks he's a bore.
(78b)   I find Harry (to be) amusing, although everyone else thinks he's a bore.

Other examples of the same tendency are given below. Although not everyone will agree with my judgments as marked, I predict that if a difference is perceived, the (b) sentences will be judged as worse than the (a) sentences.

(79a)   Our latest evidence indicates Harry to be a really incompetent plumber.
(79b)   (?)Our latest evidence indicates Harry to be a plumber in LA.
(80a)   June's track performance proved her to be agile enough for further training.
(80b)   ?June's birth certificate proved her to be a doctor of veterinary medicine.
(81a)   Maxine recognizes Sam to be more competent than Harry.
(81b)   ?Maxine recognizes Sam to be double-jointed.

Complements that are very clearly subjective rather than objective can help sentences that might be out on other grounds; for instance, the judgmental character of the complement in (82a) helps the sentence significantly, (82b) without this characteristic being unacceptable.

(82a)   John and Martha consider under the bed to be the most exciting place to experiment.
(82b)   *John and Martha consider under the bed to be dusty.

Similarly, the judgmental character of the complement in (83b) makes it more acceptable than (83a).

(83a) * This proves a giraffe to be a scavenger.
(83b) ? This proves a giraffe to be a lot smarter than we ever suspected.

Degree adverbials like *really* and the comparatives *enough* and *more . . . than* accompany judgments rather than more neutral descriptions of facts. But even when degree adverbials are not appropriate, a complement may be of the subjective, or judgmental type; a complement describing an either-or change of status can be broken up by Raising, if the change of status is based on an agreed-upon, perhaps arbitrary, standard, and thus not a matter of fact outside human manipulation. *Consider* is a nice example of a verb that can be used either to describe a mental attitude, as in (84a), or a conventionally bound decision effecting a change in status, as in (84b).

(84a) I consider Fran to be a very able translator.
(84b) Let's consider Fran to be a translator rather than a linguist for the purposes of this survey.

The fact that *consider* occurs with *that* clauses less regularly than with infinitives is no doubt related to the fact that the complement of *consider* must be about a matter of judgment, in either the mental state or more performative-like sense.

There are several performative-describing verbs that in a sense are double performatives; they always describe an act of communication, and with Raising and to be *Deletion* they further imply that the person doing the communicating is also responsible for the conventionally determined state of affairs that he is "publishing." In this sense, with Raising and *to be* deletion they represent a kind of causative. (85a) is a report of what Sam said, while (85b) is only good if Sam is a judge or someone else who has the power to confer the status of "legally insane" on someone.

(85a) Sam declared that Mary was insane.
(85b) Sam declared Mary insane.

For some people, the form without *to be* Deletion in (85c) is interpreted much more readily as parallel to (85b) than to (85a).

(85c) Sam declared Mary to be insane.

Similarly, *announce* in (86b) has more of a performative with publishing sense than it does in (86a).

(86a) Ralph announced that Joan was/is the winner.
(86b) Ralph announced Joan to be the winner.

The subjective-objective distinction discussed above is related to another characteristic of Raising-derived infinitives, that the predication in complements broken up by Raising is often viewed as a characteristic or an attribute of the entity represented by the raised NP. The distinction between a proposition that characterizes something or someone and a proposition about a more neutrally viewed state of affairs is often difficult to distinguish from the subjective-objective distinction I have made. For instance, the two statements "Harry is a pipefitter" and "Harry is a prophet" can be contrasted in the light of both distinctions. The first statement is not likely to be a judgment about Harry, nor is it likely to be viewed as describing Harry as a person; and the second statement is likely to be viewed both as a matter of judgment and as attributing non-accidental qualities to Harry. The following pairs are chosen to contrast complements that describe characteristics or attributes of the entity represented by the raised NP, and complements that describe a temporary state of affairs rather than ascribing non-temporary qualities to the entity involved.

(87a)   I know Sam to be competent in everything he does.
(87b) *I know Sam to be ready to leave now.
(88a)   Alice acknowledges her new mat knife to be handy for cutting about anything, but she still insists on using her old one.
(88b) *Alice knowledges her new mat knife to be handy, but she says she won't get it for us anyway.[3]
(89a)   I believe Myrtle to be in the pink of health.
(89b) *I believe Myrtle to be at the office.

Just as *consider* is a verb whose complement must involve a matter of judgment, *depict* is a verb whose complement typically involves ascribing attributes.

(90) Alf depicted John to be slightly shorter than Rich but not as short as Mory.

(91) shows that *depict* is a Raising verb:

(91) Alf depicted there to be a lot of moss hanging from the ceiling.

The fact that both of these verbs occur rarely, if at all, with *that* clauses, is, I believe, related to these lexically determined characteristics of their complements—namely, that the complement of *consider* typically involves a matter of judgment, and that the complement of *depict* typically involves a characterization of its subject. However, the fact that *depict* governs Raising with *there*, which, being devoid of reference, can't have any quality ascribing to it, is another indication that what I am describing are tendencies and not strictly enforced constraints on Raising.

Discourse-Related Differences

Kuno (1972) makes a four-way distinction concerning the discourse function of sentences; his classifications are *theme, contrast, exhaustive listing* and *neutral description*. In this section, I would like to use a two-way distinction between neutral descriptions and other types of clauses, neutral descriptions being clauses that do not rely on previous discourse to complete their function. For instance, the clause *firemen are sexy* is not functioning in (92) as a neutral description if characteristics of firemen are under discussion, or if the topic of conversation is sex appeal.

(92) I believe that firemen are sexy.

It is also not functioning as a neutral description if it could be used in the same context as (93):

(93) I believe that firemen are the only ones that are sexy.

nor is it functioning as a neutral description if it is used to contrast firemen with policemen or some other group. It is functioning as a neutral description, however, if what is under consideration is my beliefs, and no single part of the clause is tied to previous discourse.

I suspect that Raising does not break up neutral descriptions. The evidence I have is based on very subtle judgments, however, and although it makes sense that a proposition that is largely independent of previously given information should be put into maximal relief as a fully tensed, whole constituent clause, I have found it difficult to construct appropriate examples that people have clear judgments about.

The examples below are set in contexts that are meant to force the interpretation of the complement clause as a neutral description. I think that in every case, the (b) version with an infinitive will appear less natural than the (a) version, but although no one has disagreed with any judgments, responses have generally been lukewarmly approving.

(94)   What's new on the research scene?

(94a) Recent research has indicated that air pollution is destroying thousands of acres of timber.

(94b) Recent research has indicated air pollution to be destroying thousands of acres of timber.

(95)   When Max gets in front of a group of people, he always tries to lecture to them. What particular idea was he pushing last night?

(95a) He tried to prove that the people present were drawn together by the will of God.

(95b) He tried to prove the people present to have been drawn together by the will of God.

(96)   Why is Shirley acting so peculiar?

(96a) She believes that the revolution is getting close enough to start taking it seriously.

(96b) She believes the revolution to be getting close enough to start taking it seriously.

(97)   I hear you are an expert at interpreting tracks. What do these tracks indicate to you?

(97a) They simply show that my anteater is following a caterpillar.

(97b) They simply show my anteater to be following a caterpillar.

Since I have discussed restrictions on indefinites earlier, I have purposefully excluded them as raised NP's in the examples above; but it should be noticed here, and will be discussed later, that the scarcity of indefinites as raised NP's may be related to the resistance of neutral descriptions to Raising.

The other three categories of Kuno's four-way typology do not seem to be particularly relevant to Raising to object position with infinitives (with an exception discussed in the next section). However, it is worthwhile to point out that restrictions on Raising can*not* be stated simply in terms of "theme," at least "theme" in Kuno's sense. That is, it is not the case that only themes can be raised to object position, as is sometimes assumed. A review of Kuno's distinctions is in order here. Thematic sentences with NP subjects as themes serve to comment about the theme, which is loosely defined as something already under discussion or at least "up" in the minds of the discourse partners. Exhaustive listing sentences identify some particular of a state of affairs, event, etc., part of which it is already assumed to be shared knowledge; for instance, in (98) *John* receives an exhaustive listing interpretation if it is assumed that someone kissed Mary, and what is in question is the identity of that person.

(98) John kissed Mary.

Exhaustive listings, then, can often be paraphrased with cleft or pseudo-cleft sentences, as in (99).

(99) It was John who kissed Mary.

The notion of contrastive clause is fairly straightforward; (99) could be used as a contrastive sentence, for example, if the speaker is making a parallel between two events, as in *Fred kissed Steve, so John kissed Mary*. Subjects functioning as themes, exhaustive listings and contrasted items can all be raised freely, as I have tried to illustrate in (100–103), and subjects can be raised even when a thematic NP is in non-subject position in the complement clause, as is *her* in (103).

(100) (theme) Speaking of Larry, Mary has shown him to be incompetent.
(101) (exhaustive listing) Fran believes Tom to be the one who came in late last night.
(102) (contrast) Of the two twins, I believe Sally to be interested in people and Gertrude to be more interested in learning how to draw.
(103) Although Gail always does well, this time I believe the odds to be against her.

Stativity

It is well known that non-stative complements of proposition-embedding verbs (Postal's B-verbs) resist Raising to object position. For many speakers, Raising can take place only if there is *be* or stative *have* in the complement; others will accept stative verbs, but with infinitives only, particularly if there is an adverbial stressing the judgmental or characterizing function of the predication in the complement. Accordingly, the (a) sentences in (104) and (105) are acceptable to more people than the (b) sentences, but many speakers will accept neither, and some will accept both.

(104a) This proves the can to hold more water than we thought.
(104b) This proves the can to hold water.
(105a) His latest behavior has revealed John to admire cunning more than honesty.
(105b) His latest behavior has revealed John to admire cunning.

Although generic verbs often behave syntactically like statives, most people will not like sentences in which Raising has broken up a complement with a non-stative main verb. I have ranked the sentences in (106) in decreasing order of acceptability, but I have marked none as unacceptable because there are people who will even accept (106d).

(106a) The evidence shows Fred to be an avid streaker.
(106b) The evidence shows Fred to like streaking more than anything.
(106c) The evidence shows Fred to streak more expertly than most freshmen.
(106d) The evidence shows Fred to streak while wearing red sneakers.

Sometimes an exhaustive listing interpretation will save a particular sentence that would be bad otherwise; I find that (107), given as an acceptable sentence in Dowty (1972), is good for me only when it implies that John is the one who knows what's best, rather than that one of the characteristics I would attribute to John is that he knows what is best for the country. Kuno's exhaustive listing distinction will also be shown to be relevant for *as* constructions, later in this chapter.

(107) I believe John to know what's best for the country.

Accordingly, (108) for me is odd, since I don't interpret it as meaning that I believe that the only one who knows what's good for the country is John.

(108) I believe John to know what's good for the country.

I have examined characteristics of the complements of B-verbs that inhibit and favor Raising with infinitives. Before I examine similar characteristics with regard to *as* constructions, I will present in (109) a summary of the discussion so far, with relevant examples.

(109)
THE KIND OF COMPLEMENT THAT CAN BE BROKEN UP BY RAISING WITH INFINITIVES

Tendency	Examples
a. "Subjective" complements are more easily broken up than "objective" complements.	?When I looked in the files, I found her to be Mexican. I find Hank to be one of the most reliable dealers on the Strip.
b. Complements that characterize the subject are more easily broken up by Raising than are more neutrally viewed statements of fact.	I know Sam to be competent in everything he does. * I know Sam to be ready to leave now.
c. Neutral descriptions may resist Raising.	I hear you are an expert at interpreting tracks. What do these tracks mean to you? a. They simply show that my anteater is following a caterpillar. b. ?They simply show my anteater to be following a caterpillar.
d. Complements with non-stative predicates resist Raising.	The evidence shows Fred to be a habitual streaker. * The evidence shows Fred to streak wearing red sneakers.

As Constructions

I have so far observed that the kind of complement that is most likely to be broken up by Raising into a surface structure infinitive construction is one whose subject is a definitely referring NP, and whose predication is a judgment statively characterizing this entity, while the kind of complement that is most likely to surface as a *that* clause is a neutral description of an event or a state of affairs that is viewed as being empirically verifiable rather than a matter of judgment. The same observations hold true for *as* constructions, although verbs that govern Raising with *as* constructions are less likely to occur with *that* complements. For instance, Raising with *as* constructions is also more appropriate with matters of judgment, as shown in (110) and (111).

(110a)   We've established Harry as being a really incompetent plumber.

(110b) ?We've established Harry as being a plumber in LA.

(111a)   Sue is unwilling to recognize Sam as being more intelligent than Harry.

(111b) ?Sue is unwilling to recognize Sam as being doublejointed.

As constructions are more restricted than infinitive constructions, however, in that they are sensitive to whether a judgment is a non-intellectualized attitude, or even an emotion, or whether it is more of a consciously held opinion or intellectualized rather than sensory perception. For instance, (112a) with *consider* and an infinitive is more appropriate than (112b) with *regard* and an *as* construction, to relate a judgment formed on the basis of reasoning from empirical evidence.

(112a)   The weather experts at Cornell consider the recent testing of nuclear weapons to be responsible for the sudden dip in temperature.

(112b) ?The weather experts at Cornell regard the recent testing of nuclear weapons as being responsible for the sudden dip in temperature.[4]

However, I think that (113a) with *regard* may be more appropriate when the judgment involved is an involuntary reaction.

(113a)   I wish I could be more reasonable, but I can't seem to stop regarding Pat as (being) responsible for all my needs.

(113b) (?)I wish I could be more reasonable, but I can't seem to stop considering Pat to be responsible for all my needs.

The distinction I am making between an intellectualized perception of a fact and a less intellectualized reaction is a finer distinction than the objective-subjective distinction discussed with regard to infinitive, but I think it is similar. An objective proposition is one viewed as being true or false independently of human judgment and perception; a proposition viewed as a consciously held opinion rather than a description of an experience, is also in a sense more externalized. Another example of the finer distinction involves the verb *perceive* itself. In (114), which contains a *that* clause, *perceive* describes the intellectual perception of a fact, and the sentence is thus anomalous, since "the lake was smaller than it was" is anomalous.

(114) *I perceived that the lake was smaller than it was.

In (115), *perceive* with an *as* construction describes a sensory perception, and since one's cognitive awareness and sensory awareness can produce contradictory messages, the sentence is not anomalous.

(115) I perceived the lake as being smaller than it was.

For some people, though, (116), with an infinitive, is felt to be slightly strange; *perceive* with an infinitive is on the borderline between describing a sensory perception and a more intellectually conceived proposition.

(116) ?I perceived the lake to be smaller than it was.

The same kind of phenomenon puts into relief the previously mentioned difference between *regard* and *consider*.

(117a) I tend to regard Pauline as being more competent than she is.
(117b) ?I tend to consider Pauline to be more competent than she is.

The difference between *establish,* which for many people does not occur with *as* constructions, is also subtle but revealing. With *prove,* the truth functional status of the proposition represented by the complement is still empirically oriented, even with infinitives; that is, one can't be said to have proved something that is empirically false. However, with *establish,* the empirical truth functional status of the proposition is not as relevant as whether or not it functions as true in a given situation. For instance, (118a) is not appropriate if Mary is in fact not a habitual liar, and everyone but the jury knew it at the time, but I think (118b) might be used in such a context.

(118a) *We were careful to prove Mary to be a habitual liar in the eyes of the jury.
(118b) We were careful to establish Mary as being a habitual liar in the eyes of the jury.

(118a) is starred for the context mentioned and for a reading in which *in the eyes of the jury* is not in the proposition that was proved, that is, not in the underlying complement clause.)

Raising with *as* constructions is also more likely when the complement functions to characterize its subject, as shown in (119) and (120).

(119a)   Sam refused to acknowledge Mary as being competent at chess.
(119b) ?Sam refused to acknowledge Mary as being ready to leave.
(120a)   I regard Susie as being thoroughly trustworthy.
(120b) ?I regard Susie as being in her element here.

Furthermore, there is one subtle difference between *as* constructions and infinitives that seems to indicate that the subjectless adjunct is viewed as characterizing the raised NP to a slightly greater extent in *as* constructions than in infinitive constructions with *to*. R. Lakoff (1971) has observed that the *get* passive sometimes is used to suggest that the superficial subject has been affected by the action described, often adversely, while the *be* passive is appropriate with propositions viewed with more detachment. Lakoff's example repeated here in (121), for instance, is strange because it suggests that something was done to the program to its detriment.

(121) This program has gotten prerecorded.

The *get* passive is at least sometimes more appropriate with *as* constructions than with infinitive constructions, and I think that this suggests that complements that become infinitive constructions through Raising are viewed slightly less as characterizing or attributing a particular status to their subjects. The judgments are subtle indeed, and although I have marked the (b) examples below with a question mark, I mean only that I find them less natural than the (a) examples with a *get* passive.

(122a)   If you don't watch out, you'll get regarded as (being) just another crazy lady.
(122b) (?) If you don't watch out, you'll get considered (to be) just another crazy lady.[5]
(123a)   Early in the trial, the defendant got established as being a habitual liar.
(123b) (?) Early in the trial, the defendant got proved to be a habitual liar.
(124a)   Jim soon got recognized as being the most reliable escort.
(124b) (?) John soon got recognized to be the most reliable escort.

In discussing differences between infinitives and *that* clauses, of Kuno's four-way distinction between theme, contrast, exhaustive listing and neutral description, I used only the distinction between neutral descriptions and other types of clauses. In discussing *as* constructions, however, the concepts of theme and exhaustive listing are useful as well. For it often seems to be the case that *as* clauses are not paraphrasable by "as being something who. . .," which would be appropriate if the *as* clauses were serving only to characterize the raised, thematic NP. Rather, they will be paraphrasable by "as being the one who. . .," which is appropriate for an exhaustive listing, in which it is assumed in context that someone or something suits the predication contained in the *as* clause, and what is in question is the identity of the subject of the predication. For instance, getting an example with an *as* construction parallel to (125a) is difficult, if *the victim* and *a victim* are taken to be indefinite.

(125a)   Dr. Brown has proved June to be $\left\{ {the \atop a} \right\}$ victim of a rare blood disease.

(125b) ?Dr. Brown has established June as being $\left\{ {the \atop a} \right\}$ victim of a rare blood disease.

In a context in which what is in question is the identity of the person who has been attacked by a peculiar disease that strikes one person at a time, an *as* construction is good, I think, as in (126).

(126) Dr. Brown has established June as being the current victim of that rare blood disease you've probably read about.

The following pairs also show instances where *as* clauses are good only when the raised NP is used as an exhaustive listing.

(127a)   The inquiry has indicated John as being responsible for that accident on Thursday.

(127b) (?)*The inquiry has indicated John as being responsible for many accidents in the past.

(128a)   They're too stupid to recognize Patty as being the real leader of the outfit.

(128b)   ? They're too stupid to recognize Patty as being a real leader.

Although I accept both (129a) and (b), I have found that even with *regard,* some people prefer (129a), with an exhaustive listing, to (129b), in which the complement predication only serves to characterize the raised NP.

(129a) I regard Patty as being the real leader of the outfit.
(129b) I regard Patty as being a real leader.

As far as I know, this is not true for *consider* with infinitives, however, as in (130).

(130a) I consider Patty to be the real leader of the outfit.
(130b) I consider Patty to be a real leader.

As constructions are definitely more restricted with regard to stativity than are infinitives; significantly more people I have consulted will accept only stative *be* and *have* as gerunds in *as* constructions, than will accept only *be* and *have* with infinitive constructions. Some will accept gerunds of stative main verbs, and even gerunds of non-stative verbs, if there is other material in the complement to detract from an interpretation of the complement as factually describing an event. The sentences in (131) are given in order of decreasing acceptability, as were similar sentences with infinitives in example (106); although I have left them all unmarked, not many people will accept them all, and more people will balk at more sentences in (131) than in (106).

(131a) I regard June as being the culprit.
(131b) I regard June as having shirked her responsibilities.
(131c) I regard June as wasting her time among people like us.
(131d) I regard June as speaking French more fluently than Harold.
(131e) I regard June as speaking too often.

To summarize the facts once again, then, *that* clauses are relatively very free with regard to the kind of complement they can contain, but for Raising-derived infinitive constructions and *as* constructions, there is a tendency for the raised constituent to definitely refer to an object or person and for the surface structure adjunct to statively characterize or identify it, or at least for the clause broken up by Raising to express a judgment rather than to neutrally describe an event or an empirically verifiable state of affairs. The behavior of *as* constructions in this regard is summarized in (132).

The greater surface structure integrity of the derived SVO strings with *as* constructions than with infinitive constructions is correlated with the greater strictness of constraints for *as* constructions on what kind of complement can be broken up by Raising. While Raising with both constructions tends to break up "subjective" complements more easily than "objective" ones in both cases, Raising with *as* constructions

(132)
THE KIND OF COMPLEMENT
THAT CAN BE BROKEN UP
BY RAISING WITH *AS* CONSTRUCTIONS

Tendency	Examples
a. "Subjective" complements are more easily broken up than "objective" complements.	Sue is unwilling to recognize Sam as being more intelligent than Mary. *Sue is unwilling to recognize Susie as being double-jointed.
b. Complements viewed as presenting consciously held propositions are less easily broken up than complements describing sensory perceptions or emotions.	I perceived the lake as being smaller than it was. ?I perceived the lake to be smaller than it was.
c. Complements that characterize the subject are more easily broken up by Raising than are more neutrally viewed propositions.	I regard Susie as being thoroughly trustworthy. ?I regard Susie as being in her element here.
d. Neutral descriptions resist Raising.	Why is Shirley acting so peculiar? a. She thinks she established that the revolution is getting close enough to take seriously. b. *She thinks she's established the revolution as getting close enough to take seriously.
e. Sometimes, Raising demands an exhaustive listing reading of the complement subject.	The inquiry has established John as being responsible for that accident on Thursday. ?The inquiry has established John as being responsible for many accidents in the past.
f. Complements with non-stative predicates resist Raising.	I regard John as being the culprit. *I regard John as speaking too often.

is further limited by other subtle differences between an intellectualized and thus to some extent "externalized" proposition, and a description of a sensory or emotionally colored perception. Complements that characterize the subjects are more easily broken up by Raising with both constructions. Complements with neutral descriptions resist Raising with both constructions, and *as* constructions are sometimes further limited to complements whose subjects receive an exhaustive listing interpretation. The stativity constraints are much stricter for *as* constructions than for infinitives.

I have presented many separate but related generalizations about *that* clauses, Raising-derived infinitive constructions and Raising-derived *as* constructions. The constant hope, if not assumption, of the generative grammarian is that somewhere in a bewildering mass of obviously related facts can be found a simple, elegant generalization (or perhaps two) from which all else will follow. With regard to the data at hand, I am far from attaining this goal, but there are some gross relations I would like to point out, although what is basic and what can be predicted from what is still a problem for me.

Kuno (1972) mentions an observation in Perlmutter (1971), that in English, when the predicate is stative or habitual, it is not possible to use an indefinite noun phrase as subject. Kuno gives these examples:

(133a)   The boy is tall.
(133b)   John is tall.
(133c)   John goes to college.
(134a)   *A boy was tall.
(134b)   *Two boys were tall.
(134c)   *Two boys go to college.

If predicates of B verb complements broken up by Raising are always stative or habitual (generic), then it follows that a raised constituent won't be an indefinite noun phrase.[6]

Kuno also proposes the following hypothesis, which I quote here in (135):

(135) The subject of the sentence in English whose predicate represents a state (but not existence) or habitual action cannot receive the neutral-description interpretation.

By this generalization and the generalization that the predication in B-verb complements is always stative or habitual with Raising, then it also follows that the raised subject (and so the whole complement) cannot receive a neutral-description interpretation. It does not follow from Perlmutter and Kuno's observations that a constituent raised out of an *existential* sentence won't be an "indefinite," or non-referring, noun phrase, or that raised subjects of *existential* sentences cannot receive a neutral-description interpretation, however.

The fact that non-referential *there* in existential sentences escapes the constraints on non-referential NP's in pre-infinitival position is less arbitrary if the facts about indefinites and non-referential NP's follow from the nature of the predication in Raising-derived B-verb constructions. As to the question of whether or not Raising-derived complements containing existential sentences can receive a neutral-description interpretation, the facts again aren't clear. In contexts stressing a neutral-description interpretation of the complement, as in (136) and (137), for instance, it does seem to me that the sentences with existential complements are better than the sentences with stative or habitual predication in their complements; but given all the related facts described in this chapter, and the variety and subtlety of judgments, it is difficult to consider this to be a strong argument for anything.

(136)   When Max gets in front of a group of people, he always lectures to them. What particular idea was he trying to push last night?
(136a)   He tried to prove there to be life on Mars.
(136b)   He tried to prove the people present to have been drawn together by the will of God.
(137)   I hear you are an expert at interpreting tracks. What do the tracks indicate to you?
(137a)   They simply show there to be a struggle going on between an anteater and a caterpillar.
(137b)   They simply show an anteater to be chasing a caterpillar.

The whole question becomes unbearably complicated when one realizes that crucial terms used in Perlmutter's and Kuno's generalizations are not well-defined and very likely cannot be very neatly defined. What counts as a state or habitual action, for instance? Passive *be* and the progressive *be* act like statives, but sentences like (138) and (139), with indefinite subjects, can be neutral descriptions.

(138)   Listen! Somebody is mowing the neighbor's lawn.
(139)   Have you heard the news? An SLA member was killed by the FBI last night, but they don't know who it was.

The constraints on what kind of NP can be raised, and the stative and/or habitual nature of the predication, might both follow from a tendency for the predication of the complement clause to characterize the raised NP subject. That is, characterizing involves ascribing qualities to a referent, and predication used to ascribe qualities is stative (note that habital actions can be viewed as characterizing the actor, and that generic verbs often act like statives). In fact, this seems to be a simpler view of the mass of constraints and generalizations in this chapter, except that it does not cover the case of raised non-referential NP's like *it, there* and idiom chunks.

There is also the problem of definiteness of reference and quantifier scope. The fact that *as* constructions are more restrictive than infinitive constructions with regard to definiteness of reference of raised constituents, and the fact that quantifiers in pre-*as* position are consistently interpreted with wide scope when quantifiers in pre-*to* position are not, and the fact that in other ways pre-*to* NP's are more syntactically bound to infinitive clauses than pre-*as* NP's are bound to *as* clauses—all these facts are undoubtedly related, but I know of no reason to choose one as a more basic fact than another.

Similarly, the fact that Raising-derived adjuncts often characterize the raised NP, and the fact that *that* clauses more often describe events or states of affairs viewed neutrally both in terms of discourse context and in terms of being true or false independently of human judgment, and the fact that *that* clauses are more like independent clauses than are constructions derived by Raising—all these facts are obviously related, but precisely *how* they are related is not clear to me. The purpose of this chapter has been to point out that these relationships exist; their formalization will have to await a clearer understanding than mine of which facts are basic, and which facts naturally follow from these.

CHAPTER IV FOOTNOTES

[1] I am grateful to Adrian Akmajian for comments on a previous version of the first part of this chapter. It will be obvious that I have also benefitted from the very rich LSA paper he presented on a topic close to the topic of this chapter.

[2] David Peterson points out that in non-complex sentences, the most normal position for non-referring definite descriptions is in predicate nominal position after the copula, rather than in subject position. This is another case in which complements that resist Raising to object position are slightly marked to begin with; several people have pointed out that (ii) sounds "more natural" than (i)

    (i) From here to Los Angeles is a long way.
    (ii) It's a long way from here to Los Angeles.

Often, too, sentences that seem fine alone will slightly resist Raising to subject position but will more strongly resist Raising to object position, as in (iii):

    (iiia)   A good impression was made by several people.
    (iiib) ?A good impression is likely to have been made by several people.
    (iiic) *This shows a good impression to have been made by several people.

In other words, Raising to subject position and Raising to object position seem to be constrained similarly with regard to what kind of constituent can be raised, although Raising to subject position is a lot more free.

[3] I owe the *handy* (useful) vs. *handy* (conveniently near) test to Bolinger (1967a).

[4] I am confounded by John Lawler's observation that (i) and (ii) are equally good:

(i) The weather experts at Cornell consider the dip in temperature to be a result of the recent testing of nuclear weapons.

(ii) The weather experts at Cornell regard the dip in temperature as being a result of the recent testing of nuclear weapons.

[5]It has been called to my attention that both sentences in (122) are out for some speakers, but I have not had the opportunity to investigate why.

[6]Kuno points out 1) that the relevant interpretation of "indefinite" involves reference rather than some mechanical notion of "indefinite article," since sentences like (i) and (ii) are good,

(i) One boy that I met yesterday was tall

(ii) A friend of mine has an IQ of 160.

and 2) that indefiniteness is a non-discrete concept, since when the class in which the referents of the indefinite subjects are to be located becomes smaller, sentences like those under discussion become better.

(iii)   *A student is dumb.

(iv)   ?A student that I met yesterday was dumb.

(v)   A student in my class who has a grade average of C has an IQ of 160.

V

To Be Deletion[1] and *That* Deletion

Raising to object position with infinitive formation weakens the integrity of an underlying object complement by removing its subject, neutralizing tense distinctions and putting the remaining predication into an adjunct-like surface structure role. *To be* Deletion, the rule relating sentences like (1a) and (1b), further destroys the separate clause status of an underlying object complement.

(1a) I consider this discussion to be useless.
(1b) I consider this discussion useless.

The formation of *that* clauses, on the other hand, maintains the integrity and independence of an underlying object complement. Un-

75

like infinitive clauses, *that* clauses never lose their subjects or their tense-carrying constituent.

    (2a)   Mary, I believe (to be) insane.
    (2b) * Mary, I believe that is insane.
    (3a)   I believe Mary capable of anything.
    (3b) * I believe that Mary capable of anything.

It will be seen that complements with *that* deleted offer somewhat less resistance to movement rules across clause boundaries, although the syntactic effect of *that* deletion is much more subtle than the effect of Raising or even *to be* Deletion.

In this chapter I will show that the constraints on what kind of complement can be further broken up by *to be* Deletion echo the constraints on what kind of complement can be broken up by Raising, and that constraints on what kind of subject *that* deletion can leave juxtaposed to the matrix main verb echo the constraints on what kind of subject can be raised to object position. These facts will be presented as further evidence that the semantic and pragmatic correlates of Raising noted in the previous chapter are in fact systematically related to the surface structure consequences of Raising.

The distinction made in the previous chapter between propositions viewed as matters of human judgment and propositions viewed as empirically verifiable matters of fact is also useful with regard to *to be* Deletion; although some people will accept sentences like the (a) sentences in (4–6), in which Raising has broken up a proposition about an empirically verifiable matter of fact, I don't think that anyone will accept the (b) variants with *to be* Deletion.

    (4a) ? Why, I believe Tom to be Italian after all.
    (4b) * Why, I believe Tom Italian after all.
    (5a) ? When I looked in the files, I found her to be Mexican.
    (5b) * When I looked in the files, I found her Mexican.
    (6a) ? June's birth certificate proved her to be a doctor of veterinary medicine.
    (6b) * June's birth certificate proved her a doctor of veterinary medicine.

The sentences in (7–9) are much better than those in (4–6); the difference is that the complements broken up by Raising and *to be* Deletion are viewed as matters of judgment.

    (7) I believe Tom capable, if not astoundingly competent.

(8) I found Maxine extremely charming.

(9) June's track performance proved her agile enough for the big time.

Similarly, *understand* is used in a conjectural sense rather than expressing a judgment, in (10a), but a corresponding sentence with *to be* Deletion is not acceptable.

(10a)   I understand Frank to be willing to compromise.
(10b)   *I understand Frank willing to compromise.

Consider always describes a subjective judgment rather than a state of belief with regard to an empirically verifiable matter of fact, but the example in (11), which I owe to Michael Szamosi, shows *consider* with *to be* being more appropriate in a situation where a proposition is regarded from the standpoint of truth or falsity:

(11) I just found out that Sally isn't related to me at all, and it surprises me because I always considered her
$\begin{cases} \text{to be my sister} \\ \text{?my sister} \end{cases}$.

In contrast, the version without *to be* is more appropriate in (12), suggested to me by Arlene Berman, since *consider* here describes my feelings toward and treatment of another person, and the proposition involved has nothing to do with a literal matter of fact.

(12) I always considered him $\begin{cases} \text{part of the furniture} \\ \text{to be part of the furniture} \end{cases}$.

The subjective-objective distinction is not quite enough to describe acceptability differences in variants with and without *to be,* however. Notice that none of the main verbs in the following sentences allow *to be* Deletion:

(13a)   I know Sally to be understanding and patient.
(13b)   *I know Sally understanding and patient.
(14a)   Maxine grudgingly recognizes Sam to be more competent than Harry.
(14b)   *Maxine grudgingly recognizes Sam more competent than Harry.
(15a)   Molly disclosed Alex to be less loyal than we thought.
(15b)   *Molly disclosed Alex less loyal than we thought.

(16a)   The inquiry revealed Laura to be at fault.
(16b) *The inquiry revealed Laura at fault.
(17a)   The investigation confirmed Sally to be good at her job.
(17b) *The investigation confirmed Sally good at her job.
(18a)   We discovered Susie to be secretly in love with Studs.
(18b) *We discovered Susie secretly in love with Studs.

The examples in (19) show that these are in fact Raising verbs.

(19) Sarah ⎰ knows   ⎱ there to be more truth in
            ⎱ recognizes ⎰
              disclosed
              revealed
              confirmed
              discovered
        the rumors than Dick will admit.

It seems, then, that *to be* Deletion not only is sensitive to the
objective-subjective distinction previously discussed, but complements
broken up by *to be* Deletion must represent a self-initiated,[2] original
opinion, rather than a recognition of the truth of a proposition formed
by someone else, even a proposition that is subjective in that it concerns
a matter of judgment. The verbs *know, recognize, disclose, reveal, confirm* and *discover* all imply the uncovering or the acceptance of a fact
rather than the forming of an opinion or a perception necessarily original with the person perceiving. The conjectural *understand* is also of
this kind; although *Frank is the most amusing raconteur of the lot* most
likely expresses a judgment rather than an empirically oriented statement of fact, (20) is unacceptable. I think that this is because *understand* with an infinitive is appropriate only when the complement
contains second hand information rather than a self-initiated perception.

(20) *I understand Frank the most amusing raconteur of the lot.

The distinction between a self-initiated perception and acceptance
of a proposition formed, or at least formulable, by someone other than
the subject of the matrix verb, can also make a difference in the acceptability of sentences with full infinitives as opposed to *that* clauses;
for instance, although *believe* can be used to describe the acceptance
of the truth of a proposition presented by someone other than the
subject of the matrix clause, as in (21a), this use of *believe* is not
appropriate with infinitives at all, as shown in (21b).[3]

(21a)   The doctor$_i$ has told Sam that Mary$_j$ has leukemia, but Sam won't believe that she$_j$ is sick.
(21b)   *The doctor$_i$ has told Sam that Mary$_j$ has leukemia, but Sam won't believe her$_j$ (to be sick).

The distinction between initiating and accepting or discovering the truth of a proposition is closely linked not only to the subjective-objective distinction previously discussed, but also to whether or not a complement represents a fact based on experience or, rather, describes the experience itself. The trio of sentences with *find* in (22–24) can be viewed from this angle as well; the complement in (22), then, represents a proposition viewed as based on evidence, while the complement in (24) represents the report of an experience. I might use (22) but not (24) as a statement about consumer reaction tests, but I would use (24) and not (22) as a statement about how the chair feels to me.

(22) I find that this chair is uncomfortable.
(23) I find this chair to be uncomfortable.
(24) I find this chair uncomfortable.

(23), on the other hand, might be used in either circumstance.

Similarly, (25b) is odd because I cannot directly report a sensory experience of someone else's.

(25a)   I find sewing to be refreshing to Jane.
(25b) *I find sewing refreshing to Jane.

The word *experience* is slippery in just the right way to describe the facts of *to be* Deletion, for as well as referring to a sensory experience, it can refer to first hand evidence about factual matters, as in (26).

(26) He's had a lot of experience with phony drugs.

And this kind of experience is also relevant to *to be* Deletion; in (27), for example, the kind of direct experience that allows *to be* Deletion is direct firsthand experience forming the basis of a judgment.

(27) The doctor finds sewing good for Jane.

Similarly, (28) is good because scientists are making a judgment on the basis of direct evidence, but (29) is odd because presumably Max is just relaying facts acquired secondhand.

(28)   Scientists report the sea level down considerably from what
       it was in 1952.

(29) ? In his science essay, Max reports the sea level down consid-
       erably from what it was in 1952.

As I have observed, the characterizing vs. neutral reporting distinction drawn previously is very difficult to separate from a subjective
vs. objective distinction. I have tried to isolate the former distinction
in the following examples, which show a subtle difference in acceptability according to whether or not the complement characterizes the
raised NP, although in every case the complement would be classified
as subjective rather than objective.

(30a)   John considers her to be knowledgeable enough to handle
         the situation.

(30b)   John considers her knowledgeable enough to handle the
         situation.

(31a)   John considers her to be briefed well enough to handle
         the situation.

(31b) (?) John considers her briefed well enough to handle the sit-
         uation.

The complement in both (30) and (31) describes a judgment, but *knowledgeable* represents a non-temporary characteristic, while *briefed* represents a temporary state. *To be* Deletion is more appropriate with the
first adjective, I think. It also seems to me that *easy to clean,* which
characterizes its subject, is more likely to be juxtaposed with it by *to
be* Deletion than is *easy to reach,* which does not describe an
attribute.

(32a)   I consider this knife easier to clean than that one.

(32b) (?)I consider this knife easier to reach than that one.

In Chapter IV, I contrasted either-or, empirical matters of fact not
only with characterizations and opinions, but with matters of social
convention. There it was mentioned that *to be*-deleted complements of
announce, declare and *proclaim* force a reading in which the complement describes a conventional change of status. It also happens that
the change of status must be under the control of the subject of the
Raising verb, in such cases; the examples below bear this out.

(33a)   NBC announced Snerd (to be) the winner in its latest pop-
         ularity poll.

(33b)   The John Birch Society announced Snerd
$\begin{cases} \text{to be the winner} \\ \text{?the winner} \end{cases}$ in NBC's latest popularity poll.

(34a)   The judge declared Mary Stultz (to be) insane.

(34b) % Mrs. Grass declared Mary Stultz to be insane.

(34c) ? Mrs. Grass declared Mary Stultz insane.

(35a)   The judge found the defendant
$\begin{cases} \text{to be guilty} \\ \text{guilty} \end{cases}$ on 30 counts.

While the causative-like reading of *announce, declare* and *find* may be present with infinitives, it is out with *that* clauses. I think that (36) and (37) can only be reports of non-juridical speech acts.

(36) The judge declared that Max was insane.

(37) The judge found that the defendant was guilty on 30 counts.

This shows again, I think, that *to be* Deletion and Raising share the same constraints, or effects, but that with *to be* Deletion these constraints are clearer.

Although *prove, show, presume, suppose,* and *assume* do not typically embed complements representing judgments, they often are used in contexts in which the truth of the embedded proposition has a conventional status as a formally accepted proposition in a legal routine, or just in a chain of reasoning set up in a conversation. So, for instance, *to be* Deletion is appropriate in (38a), but not (38b), if John's mother can only speculate about the truth and not have any control over John's legal status.

(38a)   The court presumed John innocent until he was proven guilty.

(38b) ? His mother presumed John innocent until he was proven guilty.

The sentences in (39) and (40) are meant to contrast situations in which complements are viewed as valid only within the bounds of a chain of reasoning, in which case *to be* Deletion is appropriate, and sentences in which complements do not have such a conventional status, in which case *to be* Deletion is not appropriate. I assume that each of the (a) sentences below are good with a full infinitive.

(39a) * Do you suppose Lyle ready for the physical?

(39b)   Let's suppose him ready for the physical. What then?

(40a) ? I assume Mary willing to go along. What do you think?

(40b)   Let's assume Mary willing to go along. (Even so, we would
        have a hard time convincing the dwarf.)

Since proving something always involves a chain of inference, and
not a simple unwrapping of a hidden truth, *prove* allows *to be* Deletion,
even when a matter of judgment or perception is not involved.

(41) You'll have to prove Tillie able to lift 400 pounds before I'll
      believe she threw Sam off a moving roller coaster.

In the previous chapter, I suggested that complements functioning
as neutral descriptions resist Raising, but I found it difficult to get
clear examples of this. I think the facts, although still subtle, are
clearer for *to be* Deletion, however. Of the (a), (b), and (c) sentences
below, the sentences with *to be* Deletion seem strangest in a context
which forces a reading in which the complement is functioning as a
neutral description, while the (a) sentences with *that* seem most ap-
proriate.

(42)   I'm going to present a problem to you, but first let me set
       up some assumptions.

(42a) Let's assume that Mary is eager to join the Air Force.

(42b) Let's assume Mary to be eager to join the Air Force.

(42c) Let's assume Mary eager to join the Air Force.

(43)   What reason do you have to think that Gert's judgment is
       faulty?

(43a) She believes that Max is trustworthy.

(43b) She believes Max to be trustworthy.

(43c) She believes Max trustworthy.

Both Raising and *to be* Deletion break up the syntactic integrity
of object complements, and for both rules, syntactic disintegration accompanies a semantic movement from an empirically oriented or dis-
course-given, independent proposition toward a proposition viewed as
a matter of personal judgment, personal experience, or social convention. *To be* Deletion goes one step further than Raising in merging two
clauses into one. This syntactic difference is accompanied by an increasing strictness of constraints having to do with how the speaker
views the complement, how the matrix verb forces one to view it, and
what role the complement plays in the discourse. The constraints involved are summarized in (44), which compare *to be* Deletion and Raising.

(44)
CHARACTERISTICS OF *TO BE* DELETION AND RAISING

Tendencies	Examples
a. *to be*-deleted complements are more "subjective" than complements with *to be*.	?When I looked in the files, I found her to be Mexican. *When I looked in the files, I found her Mexican.
b. Verbs that govern *to be* Deletion must describe a self-initiated, original perception or opinion rather than the recognition of the truth of a proposition formed by someone else. This distinction also can affect Raising.	*The investigation confirmed Sally good at her job. *The doctor has told Sam that Mary has leukemia, but Sam won't believe her to be sick.
c. Complements with *to be* Deletion must not only describe judgments but must characterize the subject as well. Raising is affected by such distinctions but not as strongly.	Bob believes her to be briefed well enough to handle the situation. ?Bob believes her briefed well enough to handle the situation. I know Sam to be competent *to be more ready to leave than I am.
d. A causative-like reading of *announce, declare,* etc. is possible with full infinitives, but necessary with infinitives without *to be*.	Mary declared that Sue was insane. The doctor declared Sue to be insane. The judge declared Sue insane.
e. Neutral descriptions seem to resist Raising, but this resistance is clearer with *to be* Deletion.	I'm going to present a problem to you, but first let me set up a context for it. a. (?)Let's assume Mary to be eager to join the Air Force. b. ?Let's assume Mary eager to join the Air Force.

Generally, the more the predication in the underlying object complement is viewed as true or false independently of the control or perception of the subject of the Raising verb, the less likely it is that the structure of the complement will be broken up by Raising and then *to be* Deletion. Since *to be* Deletion works on the output of Raising, sentences with essentially the same lexical items and cognitive message form a continuum from the presentation of a fact viewed as empirically verifiable to the statement of an individual judgment, according to whether both Rules have applied, or only Raising has applied, or neither has applied.

That Deletion

George Lakoff has pointed out to me that *that* Deletion somewhat
weakens the islandhood of object complements; that is, it weakens the
resistance of elements in surface structure object complements to removal to a position outside the complement clause. For instance, as
shown in G. Lakoff (1973), adverb preposing can prepose elements into
higher clauses with varying degrees of freedom, depending on what
kind of adverb is being preposed and depending on where the embedding clause stands on a hierarchy of islandhood. The fact that (45b) is
better than (45a) indicates that *that* Deletion makes the object complement slightly less of an island.

(45a) ?Tomorrow, I think that I'll leave.
(45b)   Tomorrow, I think I'll leave.

Although subjects of *that* clauses are never removed, Topicalization
(or Y-Movement) can move the subject of a complement in which *that*
has been deleted.

(46a) *Mary, I believe that is genuinely ill, but John, I believe
        that is only fooling.
(46b)   Mary, I believe is genuinely ill, but John, I believe is only
        fooling.

Objects can also be moved from *that*-less complements more easily than
from complements in which *that* has been deleted.

(47a) ?This dress, I suppose that you'll want to wear home.
(47b)   This dress, I suppose you'll want to wear home.

Question formation affects subjects of *that*-less clauses but not subjects
of clauses with *that*.

(48a) ?*Just who do you think that you are, anyway?
(48b)   Just who do you think you are, anyway?

As has often been noticed elsewhere, subjects of *that* clauses can't be
relativized.

(49a) *There's the man who I thought that was following me.
(49b)   They've spotted the man who I thought Susan was follow-
        ing.

Subjects of *that*-less clauses can be relativized, however.

(50) There's the man who I thought was following me.

Clauses with *that* also seem to be less affected by the negation of an element in a higher clause; although the difference is too subtle to be sure about, I think that (51b) and (52b) are slightly better than their counterparts with *that*.

(51a) (?)I doubt that she paid a red cent for that coat.
(51b)　 I doubt she paid a red cent for that coat.
(52a) (?)I don't think that Sam is coming until Friday.
(52b)　 I don't think Sam is coming until Friday.

To some extent, then, *that* Deletion weakens the separate clause status of an object complement. Although I have found no corresponding difference in the type of predication in the complement whose independence is slightly affected by this change, Adrian Akmajian has pointed out to me that some of the restrictions on what kind of constituent can be raised to object position are paralleled by similar restrictions on what kind of constituent can serve as subject of a *that*-deleted complement.[4] He observes, for instance, that in his speech, generics, *the littlest thing,* and prepositional phrases are odd as subjects of *that*-less clauses, and has offered these examples (which I have marked according to his judgments, since I share his feeling about their acceptability relative to each other).

(53a)　 We believe that
$\left\{\begin{array}{l}\text{Fido}\\ \text{a beaver}\\ \text{any beaver}\\ \text{a beaver with any brains at all}\end{array}\right\}$
　　 is a lot smarter than any chipmunk.
(53b)　 We believe
$\left\{\begin{array}{l}\text{Fido}\\ \text{?a beaver}\\ \text{?*any beaver}\\ \text{?*a beaver with any brains at all}\end{array}\right\}$
　　 is a lot smarter than any chipmunk.
(54a)　 John believes that the littlest thing throws me into a tizzy.
(54b)　 ?John believes the littlest thing throws me into a tizzy.
(55a)　 They believed that from London to Paris was a long way.
(55b) ?*They believed from London to Paris was a long way.

Similarly, although the indefinite some (sm) can occur in some *that*-deleted complements, as in (56), it is odd in others, as in (57b) and (58b).

(56)   I think sm people are trying to get in.
(57a)   John proved that sm people were agitating for removal of the Chairman.
(57b)   ?John proved sm people were agitating for removal of the Chairman.
(58a)   Fran acknowledged that sm people were coming over for beer later.
(58b)   ?Fran acknowledged sm people were coming over for beer later.

Although the facts about *to be* Deletion and *that* Deletion presented in this chapter support my contention that the semantic and pragmatic characteristics of infinitives, *as* constructions and *that* clauses are related to the surface structure characteristics of these constructions, they do not help with the problem presented at the end of the last chapter, namely, the problem of what facts follow from what other facts. In particular, it is disappointing to me that I cannot find any differences between *that* clauses and *that*-less clauses in how the speaker views the complement, differences that would correspond to similiar differences in sentences with *that* clauses, full infinitives, and infinitives with *to be* Deletion. If the constraints on what kind of constituent can be raised to object position were a function of what kind of complement can be broken up by Raising, one would expect the similar constraints on what kind of constituent can be the subject of *that*-less clauses to be accompanied by parallel constraints on what kind of complement can appear in *that*-less clauses. But this is not the case. In fact, Bolinger's (1972) contention that *that*-less clauses are more appropriate than clauses with *that* when the matrix in the complement is being newly asserted rather than being commented on, points out a difference between infinitives and *that*-less clauses, since I have claimed in Chapter IV that infinitive clauses do not represent neutral descriptions (in Kuno's sense). Bolinger observes that object clauses carrying hedged assertions are unlikely to appear without *that;* *think, guess* and *understand* in the *that*-less sentences in (59) are more likely to be taken as conjectural verbs hedging an assertion, parallel to their use as parentheticals, than they are in the sentences with *that.*

(59a) ?I $\left\{\begin{array}{l}\text{think}\\\text{guess}\\\text{understand}\end{array}\right\}$ that it's gonna rain.

(59b) I $\left\{\begin{array}{l}\text{think}\\\text{guess}\\\text{understand}\end{array}\right\}$ it's gonna rain.

While this is interesting for the study of degrees of islandhood and rules involving indirect speech acts, it runs counter to the tendency I have noticed for Raising and *to be* Deletion not to merge complements that are viewed as newly asserted matters of fact. In short, then, the facts presented in this chapter support the point I have been making in previous chapters, but the explanation behind the facts is still elusive.

CHAPTER V FOOTNOTES

[1]Much of the material in this chapter has been presented in Borkin (1973), and I thank the Chicago Linguistic Society for permission to use it here. I would also like to acknowledge my debt to Kiparsky and Kiparsky (1971), who first explored Raising in terms of the semantics of the verbs governing Raising and their complement. Much of the information in this and the previous chapter is a more detailed examination of facts presented in their important article.

[2]Susie Andres has helped me in ferreting out this distinction.

[3]Lindholm (1969) has shown that negative-Raising is also blocked out of complements embedded under *believe* with this sense, indicating (to me, at least) that degrees of islandhood are not simply a matter of tree structure. The "acceptance" sense of believe lends a quote-like aspect to the complement, which I believe is involved in the complement's resistance to being broken up by negative-Raising and Subject Raising.

[4]Akmajian attributes to Chomsky the general observation that infinitive complements and *that*-less clauses share many peculiarities.

VI

Lexically Conditioned Constraints on Raising, and the Equi vs. Raising Alternative

Verbs that embed propositions and that govern Raising also can occur in surface structure with non-sentential objects, as in (1–3).

(1) I believe Harry.
(2) Sam knows the answer.
(3) Mabel proved the theorem.

Bolinger (1967) observed that when SVO strings derived by Raising are interpretable independently, the compatibility of the meaning of such strings with the meaning carried by the whole SVO adjunct string often influences the acceptability of the longer unit. If the message of the smaller string is incompatible with the message of the larger string that includes it, the sentence derived by Raising is somewhat suspect, as, for instance, in the examples below. (Justification that these verbs are Raising verbs will be presented later.)

(4a)   I suspect John to be dishonest, although it would appear otherwise.

(4b)   ?I suspect John to be honest, although it would appear otherwise.

(5a)   Tom confirmed the rumor to be essentially true.

(5b)   ?*Tom confirmed the rumor to be essentially false.

(6a)   The curator quickly verified the vase to be an authentic example of pre-Columbian stone work.

(6b)   ?The curator quickly verified the vase to be a fake.

(7a)   Mary proved Sam's claim to be true in most respects.

(7b)   ?Mary proved Sam's claim to be false in most respects.

(8a)   Frank suggested larceny to be the only way out.

(8b)   ?*Frank suggested larceny to be the cowardly way out.

Sometimes, the problem is that SVO strings are not compatible with other facts assumed to be true in context, rather than being incompatible with the sentence as a whole. (9b) is odd because in 1974 the statement *I know Napoleon* is inappropriate.

(9a)   I believe Napoleon to be the general most respected by contemporary military historians.

(9b)   ?I know Napoleon to be the general most respected by contemporary military historians.

In (10b), I think the problem is that the derived SVO string doesn't make as much sense alone as the SVO string in (10a).

(10a)   The salesperson then demonstrated the product to be extremely soothing to plants suffering from transplant shock.

(10b)   ?The salesperson then demonstrated warm rain to be extremely soothing to plants suffering from transplant shock.

The same factor seems to influence judgments about sentences with *estimate* discussed in Postal (1974). Postal observes that the NP occuring in object position after *estimate* must be either a non-referential, grammatically introduced element like *it* and *there*, as in (11) and (12), or an NP whose head designates the dimension of estimation, as in (13) and (14). (All the examples in [11–17] below are Postal's.)

(11)   I estimate it to be raining about two inches per hour.
(12)   I estimate there to be two million people in that valley.
(13)   I estimate the length of Bill's boat to be 36 feet.
(14)   I estimate the weight of that beam to be 47 tons.
(15)   *I estimate Bill's boat to be 36 feet long.
(16)   *I estimate that beam to weigh 47 tons.
(17)   *I estimate your sister to weigh 250 pounds.

In many cases, then, SVO strings have some kind of semantic effect as constituents, and the adjunct often seems to be expanding or qualifying a basic message carried by the SVO string. Yet these SVO strings are best analyzed as derived rather than underlying strings, since by the *there*-Raising argument presented in Chapter II, the verbs in them are Raising verbs. Sentences (18–26) show this, since I see no principled way of distinguishing the verbs in (18–26) from the same verbs in examples with meaningful derived SVO strings.

(18)   We believe there to be two few people interested in the noble sport of falconry.
(19)   He guessed there to be 44 marbles in the box.
(20)   I suspect there to be more than one person here interested in mutiny.
(21)   Tom confirmed there to be more than enough people for a quorum.
(22)   The curator quickly verified there to be enough woof left in the carpet to support a good restorative weaving job.
(23)   Mary proved there to be more than four sumkins in a gebhart.
(24)   Frank suggested there to be more money in the trust fund than Grantley was willing to admit.
(25)   I know there to be more to this affair than meets the eye.
(26)   The salesperson demonstrated there to be enough oil in the can to last through several overhaulings.

It appears, then, that Raising is blocked 1) when the SVO string derived by Raising is independently derivable as an independent and meaningful sentence; 2) when the meaning of the independently derivable SVO string is contradicted by the larger sentence in which the derived SVO string is a part; and even sometimes 3) when the independently derivable SVO string is not appropriate in the context in which the larger sentence is being used. Furthermore, to handle the cases where *there* and other dummy NP's can be raised, it must be stated that these conditions apply only when the potentially raisable NP refers.[1] The cases discussed here, then, are similar to the case discussed in Chapter II, in which Question Formation is blocked out of picture noun genitives in object position if the meaning of the derived SVO string is incompatible with the unquestioned sentence as a whole.[2]

As might be expected, constraints on Raising having to do with the semantics of derived SVO strings are more apparent with *as* clauses than with infinitives. Judgments vary with regard to the sentences with infinitives that I have marked as odd in (4–10), but I think that everyone will agree that the starred sentences in (27–30) are much worse than those.

(27a)   Tom confirmed the rumor as being essentially true.
(27b)   *Tom confirmed the rumor as being essentially false.
(28a)   We've established Sam's claim as being true in most respects.
(28b)?* We've established Sam's claim as being false in most respects.
(29a)   I just accepted it as being true that he had been here before.
(29b)   *I just accepted it as being false that he had been here before.
(30a)   I estimate the length of Bill's boat as being 36 feet long.
(30b)   *I estimate Bill's boat as being 36 feet long.

Pairs of sentences with active and passive complements often put into relief the semantic as well as syntactic integrity of SVO strings. In the sentences below, the SVO strings can be taken as meaningful independently, and only when the adjuncts can be interpreted as expanding on this message are the sentences good.

(31a)   Frank $\begin{Bmatrix} \text{disclosed} \\ \text{revealed} \end{Bmatrix}$ Cyril as having murdered Agatha.

(31a≠b) *Frank $\begin{Bmatrix} \text{disclosed} \\ \text{revealed} \end{Bmatrix}$ Agatha as having been murdered by Cyril.

(32a)   The biography depicts King as admiring Gandhi.

(32a≠b) ?The biography depicts Gandhi as being admired by King.

(33a)   Nicol described Walter as hating his wife.

(33a≠b)?*Nicol described Walter's wife as being hated by him.

(34a)   Maxine mistakenly perceived the doorman as listening intently to the music.

(34a≠b) *Maxine mistakenly perceived the music as being listened to by the doorman.

An obvious response to these examples is to suspect that they are
not derived by Raising at all, since one of the traditional tests for
Raising is the truth functional equivalence of active and passive variants of the complement. Yet the examples below show sentences with
the same main verbs and active and passive variants that are truth
functionally equivalent and equally acceptable. Whatever differences
there may be in the following sentences, they are discourse-related and
well below the level traditionally tolerated in Raising pairs.

(35a) Frank startlingly {disclosed/revealed} Cyril as having garotted
Agatha with a tiny silver wire.

(35b) Frank startlingly {disclosed/revealed} Agatha as having been garotted by Cyril with a tiny silver wire.

(36a) The Homeowner's Association depicted the neighborhood
as being about to be destroyed overnight by the blockbusters.

(36b) The Homeowner's Association depicted the blockbusters as
being about to destroy the neighborhood overnight.

(37a) Reporters described the pie as hitting the guru squarely
in the fact.

(37b) Reporters described the guru as being hit squarely in the
face by the pie.

(38a) Maxine mistakenly perceived the music as bothering the
doorman.

(38b) Maxine mistakenly perceived the doorman as being bothered by the music.

The difference between the examples in (31–34) and those in (35–38)
is that in the latter examples, attention is being focussed away from
one or another participant, toward some other aspect of the complement—toward the actual means of murdering in (35), for example, or
toward an event as a whole, as in (36).

When confusion in the Equi vs. Raising choice has been noticed
previously by transformational grammarians, it has been with verbs
embedding complements describing unrealized events or states of affairs (*want, expect, allow*), and it has been proposed that the verbs
involved govern both Raising and Equi. Bresnan (1972), for example,
proposes that *want* in the sense of "want of someone that he or she do

something" and *expect* in the sense of "putting an obligation on someone to do something" both govern Equi, although *want* and *expect* are
also both Raising verbs. In such cases, an attempt has been made to
link the Equi-raising difference to different senses of the same lexical
item. But for the troublesome cases here, it is difficult to isolate different senses of the same verb; it seems *ad hoc* to claim that *perceive,*
for instance, has a different sense when what is focussed on is the
perception of an action or event than it does when what is focussed on
is the perception of an individual person or object.

In view of the constraints already seen to be necessary to block
Raising in cases where particular verbs restrict possible derived SVO
strings, it seems plausible that, as Postal suggests, many verbs heretofore considered Equi-governing may in fact be Raising-governing,
but with constraints on Raising. It would be consonant with this approach, then, to treat many of the same verbs as taking complements
even when they occur superficially without them, as in (39–41).

(39) I believe Joan.
(40) We confirmed the rumor.
(41) Fran described the guru.

In other words, B-verbs would consistently be object-embedding in underlying structure, even though superficially they occur in a wide variety of surface constructions. In this approach 1) differences in focus,
2) what seem to be different senses of the same verb, and 3) the variety
of surface structure constructions, would all be related to pragmatic,
presuppositional and other constraints on Raising and clause-merging
such as those discussed in Chapters IV and V. All the sentences in (40)
would then be derived from an underlying structure with an object
complement, the sentences in (a–c) being derived by Raising.

(40a) Maxine described them.[3]
(40b) Maxine described them as being more interested in feeding
       themselves than in getting to their destination.
(40c) Maxine described them to be more interested in feeding
       themselves than in getting to their destination.
(40d) Maxine described how they were more interested in feeding
       themselves than in getting to their destination.

(40d) describes a situation viewed more neutrally than viewed as a
characterization, while the predication of the complements in (c) and
(b) is viewed as characterizing the underlying subject. In (40a), the
predication of the complement is left unspecified; all (40a) states is

that Maxine made some statement or statements about "their" character or appearance.

The verb *characterize* (or its prelexical counterpart), then, would' occur in exactly the same kind of underlying structure as *describe,* and the fact that *characterize* superficially occurs only in SVO strings with *as* or without an adjunct would follow from the fact that this verb is appropriate only when the predication of the complement is viewed as describing or characterizing its subject.

(41a)   Maude characterized Annie.
(41b)   Maude characterized Annie as being overly interested in the affairs of her coworkers.
(41c)   ?*Maude characterized Annie to be overly interested in the affairs of her coworkers.
(41d)   *Maude characterized $\begin{Bmatrix} \text{how} \\ \text{that} \end{Bmatrix}$ Annie was overly interested in the affairs of her coworkers.

Similarly, *suspect* could in this framework always represent an object-embedding predicate, and Raising would be linked to not only a characterization of the raised subject, but to an increasing indication that the underlying subject is faulty or suspect in a particular situation. (4a), (4b), (20), (42a) and (42b) would all be derived by Raising;

(4a)   I suspect John to be dishonest, although it would appear otherwise.
(4b)   ?I suspect John to be honest, although it would appear otherwise.
(20)   I suspect there to be more than one person here interested in mutiny.
(42a) I suspect Fran as being the real culprit.
(42b) *I suspect those observations as being relevant to the case.

(4b), then, would be odd for the same reason as (42b) is completely unacceptable, rather than a Raising-derived (4b) being odd because of some sort of surface structure constraint and an Equi-derived (42b) being unacceptable because of the logical infelicity of an underlying structure schematized in (43).

(43) I suspect those observations (those observations are relevant to the case)

The difference in degree of unacceptability between (4b) and (42b) would be related to a strictness of presupposition linking with a degree of integrity of SVO strings, although the reason for nonreferential *there* in (20) not being as affected as other NP's by presupposition linking would still be a mystery.

What are often described as "different senses of the same verb," then, would be in this framework presuppositions associatable with the same logical core. Lexically peculiar presuppositions such as that noted for *suspect* can be systematically related to surface structure syntactic differences along a one clause-two clause continuum. The sentences above with *suspect* would not differ essentially in underlying structure, for *suspect* would always represent a two-place, object-embedding predicate, and presuppositional peculiarities of *suspect* would be related to syntactic processes having the effect of merging two underlying clauses into one in surface structure. Such an approach was first suggested in Postal (1974), and although it deserves more critical scrutiny than will be leveled here, I think it is at least appealing in that it avoids the Equi vs. Raising dilemma presented in this chapter.

In this framework, an adjunct's being interpreted as expanding on or qualifying a basic message carried by the superficial SVO string is to be expected. Underlying object complements can be almost completely obliterated by removing their subject by Raising, and by deleting their predications, as has happened in (44) and (45):

(44) John described Mary.
(45) James verified the claim.

but deletion of complement predication would be possible only when that predication is unspecified or is entirely predictable from the particular verb. Thus, in (43) it is stated that John made an assertion or a series of assertions about Mary's appearance or personality, but just what he said is left unspecified. In (44), James made an assertion about a claim, but not just any assertion—he must have said that it was true. More specific information will surface in an adjunct if Raising takes place, since such information cannot be deleted; so in (46) and (47), the adjunct does in fact serve to expand or qualify a message that can be carried by the SVO string alone.

(46) John described Mary as hawk-eyed but jolly.
(47) James verified the claim as being true in essence, if not in detail.

In such a framework, it would not be necessary to relate the difference between (48a) and (49a), repeated below, to an either-or difference in underlying structure such as that implied by an Equi vs. Raising analysis.

>   (48a)   Nicol described Walter as hating his wife.
>   (48a≠b) *Nicol described Walter's wife as being hated by him.
>   (49a)   Reporters described the pie as hitting the guru squarely in the face.
>   (49a=b) Reporters described the guru as being hit squarely in the face by the pie.

Rather, pairs like these would both be derived by Raising, and differences in the degree to which the raised NP functions as a direct object in the matrix clause or a "vestigal" subject of the complement clause would have to be related to pragmatic factors like how strong the predication in the complement is viewed as being a judgment about or as characterizing its former subject.

The approach just sketched is compatible with a theory of grammar such as that alluded to in G. Lakoff (1973) and discussed by him in lectures given at the 1973 LSA Summer Institute, a theory in which logical structure is related to surface structure by wellformedness conditions that also take into account contextual and pragmatic information, and in which there is no separate level of "deep structure" such as that in the theory in which the Equi vs. Raising distinction was first formulated by Rosenbaum (1967). I have not intended that an elaboration and defense of either theory be within the scope of the present work. However, a consideration of facts first presented in Bolinger (1967b) and elaborated on here, should convince the reader that, at least for the verbs discussed in this chapter, a standard, either-or, Equi vs. Raising distinction 1) cannot be drawn on principled grounds, and 2) would crudely parallel subtle differences that have already been shown to be related to a superficial merging of two underlying clauses into one.

CHAPTER VI FOOTNOTES

[1]A similar conditional constraint (applicable only when the NP involved refers) on sentences with *there*-Doubling has been suggested by G. Lakoff to deal with sentences like (i) and (ii).

>   (i) Fran seems like she's going to faint.
>   (ii) There seems like there's gonna be a riot.

Such sentences were first noticed by Rogers (1973) and are further discussed in Rogers (1974).

[2]Formal machinery to handle these cases is available in a theory of Generative Semantics as worked on by G. Lakoff; in fact, Lakoff has suggested a possible formalization of these generalizations, but I have not had the time to responsibly present his suggestions here.

[3]A crucial question obviously arises: What is the nature of the underlying complement of *describe* and other B-verbs that appear superficially in single SVO strings? The question will remain unanswered here, although one possibility is an indirect question on the order of "what they were like" for *describe* in (40), and "what he says/said" for *believe* in (i).

    (i) I believe John.

VII

Concluding Remarks

In this monograph I have examined several types of surface structure configurations derived from an underlying two-clause, object-embedded structure, and I have shown that semantic and pragmatic correlates of rules deriving these constructions are systematically related to the surface structure consequences of these rules, all of which contribute in some degree toward the merging of an underlying two-clause structure into a superficial structure that is more like one clause. The study has been limited primarily to English constructions in which the main verb can be informally characterized as embedding clauses containing propositions as opposed to actions or events.

Recent work on causatives by Shibatani (1974) and Givon (1975) also shows semantic and pragmatic factors related to surface one clause-two clause continuums. With regard to causatives, the appropriate generalization for English seems to be that processes breaking down a two-clause separation with these verbs are related to viewing a causative situation as a single event rather than two separate events, the causing event or the agent involved in this event directly acting upon an object or person viewed as undergoing a change of state. For instance, although one of the main points of Shibatani's dissertation is that a productive vs. nonproductive distinction among causative forms is more relevant to viewing differences than are formal morphological and syntactic criteria, Shibatani points out that in English it is the case that lexical causatives like *kill, grow,* and *move* are more appropriate than constructions with two surface verbs like *cause to die, cause to grow,* and *cause to be moved* when there is direct manipulation of the entity undergoing a change. Shibatani cites the pair of sentences in (1) as examples:

(1a) John made the chair move.
(1b) John moved the chair.

(1b) would be more appropriate if John has picked up the chair, while (1a) is more appropriate if something John did has more remotely caused the chair to move or be moved.

In a Generative Semantics framework, both (1a) and (1b) would be derived from an underlying structure with an object complement[1] describing a change of state (the chair moved) and a causative pro-verb, although the underlying complement structure is superficially evident only in (1a). While both Shibatani and Givon are against such an analysis, partly on the basis of semantic and pragmatic differences like those evident in (1), G. Lakoff has suggested that such differences could be expressed as presuppositional constraints on lexicalization. In this case, then, the complex of semantic primes underlying *move* in (1b), one of which would be a predicate of causation, could be lexicalized as *move* only if the speaker assumes that the causation was direct rather than indirect (however this distinction is to be formalized).

This approach appears reasonable when it is noticed that direct and indirect manipulation, permission or persuasion are also linked to superficial syntactic differences which are more obviously related to a transformational merging of a two-clause structure. A very subtle instance of this kind is discussed by Erades (1950), who credits F. Wood with noticing that *help* followed by a plain verb stem does not mean precisely the same as *help* followed by *to* and an infinitive. I quote Erades[2]:

> In the construction with the plain verb stem the idea is that the helper participates in the activity, takes part of the work upon him, relieves the person helped of a certain amount of the work by doing it himself. Thus *will you help me get these letters addressed?*

can only mean one thing, viz, will you share with me the work of addressing them? Similarly: *I helped him mount his stamps.*

But in *will you help me to get these letters addressed?* the help may be afforded by some other means, such as relieving the speaker of other duties or tasks, e.g. *if you will attend to the telephone for a while, that will help me to get these letters addressed.*

In other words, *to* can be deleted after *help,* but when it is, this syntactic step toward the further merging of two underlying clauses is accompanied by an assumption of more direct assistance and a viewing of the act of helping and the act of something accomplished as one event rather than two. The examples in (2) and (3) show this too, I think.[3]

(2a)   Jack was so drunk he couldn't walk, so I helped him get into the car.

(2b) (?) Jack was so drunk he couldn't walk, so I helped him to get into the car.

(3a)   Give Mary a job, and help her to get into college.

(3b)   ? Give Mary a hand, and help her to unfasten that buckle.

Notice also that *get* can be deleted only when direct physical assistance is involved.

(4)   I helped him into the car by holding his elbows.

(5)   ? Your creating a disturbance helped him into the car without being seen.

Similarly, of the permissive causatives *let* and *allow,* only the latter occurs with full infinitives, and implies slightly less direct permission.[4] While in most circumstances, for instance, (6a) and (6b) are interchangeable, I think that (6a) is more appropriate if someone is being requested only to give permission remotely as the top person in a chain of command, while (6b) would be more appropriate if a jailer is being requested to open a cell.

(6a)   Will you allow them to go?

(6b)   Will you let them go?

There is some hope, then, of relating Shibatani's and Givon's observations about differences between lexical and periphrastic causatives in English to more general differences involved with the syntactic merging of two underlying clauses into one, although Shibatani's observation that in Japanese similar differences are not related to syntactic form but rather to productivity of affixes must be recognized and accounted for.

Whatever can be said about the observations and generalizations set forth in this dissertation, it cannot be said that they are very elegant, or even very neat. That is, the tendencies that have been pointed out are only tendencies—they have exceptions, and even for the same speaker, virtually no two lexical items act exactly alike with regard to the various generalizations set forth here. There are several possible explanations for this variation; at one extreme, I may not have found the few elegant generalizations that lurk behind the seemingly various data, and at the other extreme, the language itself may be chaotic. Since the first extreme implies ineptness on the part of the investigator and the second extreme implies the futility of research, I am reluctant to entertain either of these opposites. It has occurred to me, however, that I have stumbled into an area of syntax and semantics that is inherently unstable—that is, that I am investigating an area of change in progress, although I do not know just what changes are currently taking place. According to Visser (1973), the *accusative (objective) + infinitive* construction occurred in Old English with causative main verbs and has since proliferated with other semantic classes, but I have no idea whether it is now on the wane or still proliferating, and have made no study of how the change took place and what relationship it might have to the synchronic rule of *to be* Deletion. As constructions with gerunds are comparatively neglected by grammarians, but my guess about these is that they are increasing—that people who allow gerunds with verbs other than *have* and *be* are in the vanguard, and that people who allow *have* and *be* with gerunds are more in the forefront of change than people who prefer no gerunds, as in (7) and (8).

(7) I regard him as handsome.
(8) We've established him as innocent.

Although this speculation, if true, in a sense legitimizes the variation I have found, it does not reduce the importance of this variation for syntactic and semantic theory; for I assume that no one would suggest, for instance, that in constructing a synchronic theory we ignore the infinitive constructions discussed in this dissertation since they seem to be in the same state of flux that such constructions have been in for centuries. I have no answer to the dilemma posed for generative theory by synchronic and diachronic variation, but I think it is appropriate to end this dissertation by calling attention to it; and

I hope that some day the variability of the data examined here will be useful as support for a future theory, rather than presenting the obstacle that it does now to neat, simple formalization.

CHAPTER VII FOOTNOTES

[1]And with an event subject complement as well, CAUSE being a two-place atomic predicate as argued in Dowty (1972).

[2]This is from number two of Volume XXXI, p. 123.

[3]As far as I can recall, I owe this examples to Fred Lupke.

[4]I owe this observation to George Lakoff.

Appendix A

Coreference and Beheaded NP's*

Postal has suggested that sentences like the following involve a type of deletion rule:

(1) Sam weighs 250 pounds.
(2) Hanoi has refused to cooperate.
(3) IBM is greatly overpriced.

In these sentences, *Sam* refers to Sam's body; *Hanoi,* to the government whose capital city is Hanoi; and *IBM,* to the stock of the IBM company. Postal would have the surface structure NP's *Sam, Hanoi* and *IBM* in the sentences above derived from their underlying semantic representation by a deletion rule, which he refers to variously as body-deletion, government-deletion, euphemistic genital deletion, stock-deletion, etc., depending upon the semantic material involved. Accepting Postal's analysis as a framework in which to discuss such phenomena, I will refer to all such deletions as *head deletions,* and to the NP's remaining after such deletions as *beheaded NP's.*

Under the proposed analysis, then, each of the pairs of sentences in (4–7) would share the same underlying structure, the (a) sentences related to the (b) sentences by a rule deleting the head of an underlying NP.

(4a) Turn up the hi-fi.
(4b) Turn up the sound of the hi-fi.
(5a) I'm parked in a no-parking zone.
(5b) My car is parked in a no-parking zone.
(6a) Chomsky is too complicated for freshmen to read.
(6b) Chomsky's writings are too complicated for freshmen to read.
(7a) This can is contaminated.
(7b) The contents of this can are contaminated.

When two NP's beheaded by deletions of different underlying structures are coreferential in their position in underlying structure, they may function as coreferential in derived structure; and this often occurs even though the larger NP's of which they are only a part in underlying structure are not themselves coreferential. That is, if two NP's remaining after two separate deletions of two different underlying structures are coreferential before these deletions, they may continue to function as coreferential with regard to certain syntactic processes. In sentence (8), for example, reflexivization has taken place, although *Max* refers to a person, and *himself* refers to that person's genitals. In (9), *Norman Mailer* refers to a particular person, while the NP deleted by *Equi NP Deletion* must refer to the writings of that person; and in (10), pronominalization has occurred, although *Boston* refers to the physical environment of the city of Boston, and the pronoun *it* refers to the group of people that pass laws concerning that city.

(8) Max is playing with himself again.
(9) Norman Mailer doesn't mind being read under the influence of drugs.
(10) Because Boston is so dirty, it will soon enact a new anti-litter law.

NP's coreferential in their pre-head deletion position in underlying structure but beheaded by different head deletions do not always behave as coreferential with respect to rules involving coreferential NP's, however. Each of the pairs of sentences in (11–14) contain an unacceptable sentence resulting from at least two head deletions, a pair of beheaded NP's having then operated as coreferential in a transformational rule.[1]

(11a)   The campus of the University of Michigan, whose students took to the streets in a pitched battle with police last spring, will soon be all glass and steel and concrete.

(11b)   * Michigan, which took to the streets in a pitched battle with police last spring, will soon be all glass and steel and concrete.

(12a)   The government of North Vietnam wants the city of Hanoi to become more spacious.

(12b)   * Hanoi wants to become more spacious.

(13a)   The people whose work is connected with the Stock Exchange threw ticker tape all over Wall Street.

(13b)   * Wall Street threw ticker tape all over itself.

(14a)   All the people who live in the apartment house have hepatitis, and *it* badly needs a new coat of paint.

(14b)   * The whole apartment house has hepatitis, and *it* badly needs a new coat of paint.

In (11b), the beheaded NP *Michigan,* subject of the VP *will soon be all glass and steel and concrete,* has infelicitously operated as coreferential with another beheaded NP *Michigan,* subject of the relative clause VP *took to the streets in a pitched battle with police last spring.* In (12b), if the beheaded NP *Hanoi* is to represent the government whose capital is at Hanoi and if this NP acts as controller in Equi NP Deletion to delete a beheaded NP representing the city of Hanoi, the sentence is not acceptable. That is, (12b) cannot mean the same thing as (12a). In (13b), it is reflexivization between two beheaded NP's that is at fault. (14a) is good, but in (14b), the phrase *the whole apartment house,* which refers to the house's occupants, cannot act as antecedent for the pronominalization of an NP referring to the apartment house building.

Whatever the conditions may be for coreferentiality with respect to pronominalization, relative clause formation, Equi NP Deletion and reflexivization, these processes do not act uniformly with respect to NP's beheaded by deletions of different underlying structures. Although in the sentences in (15–17) the same two head deletions seem to have operated in each group, the relative acceptability of the sentences varies.

(15a) *Norman Mailer is reading himself on a nationwide TV broadcast.

(15b) Norman Mailer wants to be read on a nationwide TV broadcast.

(15c) Norman Mailer, who is seldom read on nationwide TV, will be reading someone else's work on NBC Sunday.

(16a) *The hospital decided to have itself repainted.

(16b) *The hospital wants to be repainted.

(16c) The hospital that was completely repainted last week has since reported four cases of patients being poisoned from lead fumes.

(16d) *The hospital fired Sam several weeks after it was repainted.

(17a) *Wall Street threw ticker tape on itself.

(17b) *Wall Street wants to cross Fifth Avenue.

(17c) *Yesterday my cab stalled on Wall Street, which seems to be getting panicky.

(17d) I drove along Wall Street last Friday afternoon, and I had a hard time realizing that it was in a panic.

In (15a), reflexivization is not acceptable (to me) under identity between the subject NP *Normal Mailer* and an object NP referring to the writings of Norman Mailer. However, in (15b), which is acceptable to me, Equi NP Deletion has operated to delete an NP referring to the writings of Norman Mailer under identity with the higher subject NP *Norman Mailer*. Relative clause formation in (15c) and pronominalization in (15d) have occurred under the same kind of identity as Equi NP Deletion in (15b), but the acceptability of (15d) is more doubtful to me than that of (15c). In the starred sentences (a), (b), and (d) of (16), reflexivization, Equi NP Deletion and pronominalization each result in odd sentences, but relative clause formation in (c) is acceptable; in all cases, however, the underlying pre-head deletion main subject is not the same as the other underlying NP. These examples are representative of many I have examined in that they indicate that the coreference conditions for reflexivization are often more stringent than those for Equi NP Deletion, and in turn the conditions for these two processes appear to be more stringent than those for relative clause formation and pronominalization.

I have no idea how to describe these conditions, nor am I certain why conditions on reflexivization and Equi NP Deletion should be stricter than those for the other two processes.[2] It is possible that since reflexivization, the most constrained of the four processes, occurs when two NP's command each other, and since Equi NP Deletion, the next most constrained rule, occurs when one NP commands another in the next lowest S, varying acceptability of derivations with head deletions and processes involving coreference might be explained in terms of the command relationship. Something like this seems to be to be operating in the acceptability of (17d), in which the pronoun *it* is far from being commanded by the antecedent *Wall Street*. However, relative clause formation also involves one NP commanding another in surface structure, and the following sentences show that, as far as pronominalization is concerned, acceptability of sentences with beheaded NP's is not related in any simple way to the precedence and command relationships. In every sentence in (18), the NP *Monaco* precedes and commands the pronoun *it,* but the degree of acceptance of these three sentences varies.

(18a   * Monaco realizes that it is charming.
(18b)   ? Monaco boasts that it is charming.
(18c)   Monaco regrets that it is too small in area to accommodate more millionaires.

Similarly, the sentences in (19) vary in acceptability, although in every case the pronoun *it* is not commanded by its antecedent.

(19a)   * Right after Kingston sat down at the conference table, it slid into the water.
(19b)   ? The Vatican didn't join in the festivities because it was flooded.
(19c)   Even if Monaco were larger in area, it wouldn't accept deserters.

Coreference conditions for a rule of Equi NP Deletion are particularly interesting. For example, in (20a) and in (21a), the deleted NP's cannot be simply *Harry* and *Sara,* since *merge* and *disband* take only underlying group subjects. (20b) is good only in a context where it is clear that *Harry* is used to refer to something like *the organization that Harry runs,* and I find (21b) unacceptable with any reading. The deleted subject of bomb in (22a) could be *Sally,* if Sally wanted to fly over Hanoi herself and drop bombs, but this sentence is more likely to be taken to mean that Sally wants representatives of some organization or society to which she belongs to do the bombing.

(20a)   Harry wanted to merge, but the rest of the board voted for continued separation of the two companies.
(20b)   Harry merged.

(21a)   Sara voted to disband.
(21b)   *Sara disbanded.
(22a)   Sally is really a hawk; she wants to bomb Hanoi.
(22b)   Sally bombed Hanoi last night.

There must be some sort of coreferentiality involved in these deletions, since in (20a), *Harry* must refer to a person who is a member of the organization that is the deleted logical subject of *merge, Sara* in (21a) must refer to a member of the group that is the logical subject of *disband,* and in (22a) *Sally* cannot refer to a citizen of Canada if the logical subject of *bomb* is a representative or representatives of the military organization of the United States. In a recent paper, Lawler suggests that such deletions are manifestations of government-deletion and discusses other very interesting examples of this phenomenon. He points out, for example, that (23a), (23b) and (24a) are ambiguous, but that (24b) is not.

(23a)   Nixon wants to bomb Hanoi.
(23b)   Nixon tried to bomb Hanoi.
(24a)   Mary wants to bomb Hanoi.
(24b)   Mary tried to bomb Hanoi.

That is, (23a), (23b), and (24a) are open to two readings, one in which the subject of *bomb* is one or more representatives of the United States government and one in which the subject is Nixon himself or (in [24a]) Mary herself. (24b), however, is not ambiguous if Mary is not in a power position in any government or group. One might predict that (25a) and (25b) would be equally ambiguous, the subjects of the complements being understood alternatively as Nixon personally and representatives of the government which Nixon heads.

(25a)   Nixon decided to bomb Hanoi.
(25b)   Nixon decided to walk on the moon.

However, I find a great deal of difficulty in accepting (25b) in any context other than the case where Nixon himself was or is to walk on the moon. These examples, as well as the two earlier ones (18) and (19), illustrate the fact that acceptability judgments cannot be predicted solely with respect to a particular rule and NP's beheaded by a particular pair of different head deletions. The sentences in (26–29) furnish further examples of NP's that have the same surface structure form after separate deletions of two different underlying structures behaving regularly as coreferential with respect to a certain process in one derivation but not in another.

(26a)   Dylan Thomas listened to himself being read by Richard Burton for about two minutes, and then he stood up and lumbered out of the theatre.

(26b) ?* Dylan Thomas always liked to read himself aloud to an admiring audience.

(26c) * I once heard Dylan Thomas read himself.

(27a)   Sam is redecorating the club that refused to take him as a member.

(27b) % The church that refused to take Sam as a member stands on the corner of Hollywood and Vine.

(27c) * Sam is building a steeple on the church that refused to take him as a member.

(28a)   Andy Warhol is worth more on the open market than he was before Valerie Solanis shot him.

(28b) % Chagall is worth more than Pollock on the open market because he is Jewish.

(29a)   The hospital contracted to be rebuilt without glass windows.

(29b) % The hospital refused to be rebuilt without glass windows.

(29c) ?* The hospital refused to be painted green.

It is very rare to find an acceptable sentence in which a beheaded NP whose underlying structure refers to the government whose capital is at a certain city acts as co-referential to a beheaded NP whose underlying structure refers to the government of that city or even to the city itself. For example, the earlier sentence (12b) is acceptable to me only with the reading that the Hanoi city government wants the city of Hanoi to become more spacious. And I accept (30) only if *Hanoi* refers to the government of North Vietnam, not to the city of Hanoi.

(12b)   Hanoi wants to become more spacious.

(30)   I agree with Hanoi, but I wouldn't want to live there.

Yet even this modest generalization will not hold in all cases, as Kenneth Hill has pointed out with sentence (31) and Michael O'Malley has pointed out with sentence (32):

(31)   I disagree with Hanoi and I hope we bomb it if we can spare the surrounding countryside.

(32) Washington gives me all my grants, but I wouldn't want to live there.

In head-deletion sentences, the choice of pronominal forms is solved differently by different people and in some sentences any solution is felt to be awkward. Since in English, pronouns are marked for number and gender, and relative pronouns are marked for an animate-inanimate distinction, the problem is whether pronouns will agree with the surface structure NP or with an NP deleted by a head deletion. The sentences in (33–35) illustrate differences and difficulties in pronoun agreement:

(33a) Homer is difficult to read, isn't $\begin{Bmatrix} \text{he} \\ \text{it} \end{Bmatrix}$?

(33b) Sappho is difficult to read, isn't $\begin{Bmatrix} \text{?she} \\ \text{?it} \end{Bmatrix}$?

(34)   The museum has decided to rid $\begin{Bmatrix} \text{\%themselves} \\ \text{\%itself} \end{Bmatrix}$ of cockroaches.

(35)   Washington refused to negotiate, didn't $\begin{Bmatrix} \text{\%they} \\ \text{\%it} \end{Bmatrix}$?

An inanimate-animate conflict in underlying forms of two NP's involved in relative clause formation is usually resolved in favor of the gender of the surface form, however, as shown in the next two pairs (36) and (37), and (38) and (39).

(36) Homer, $\begin{Bmatrix} \text{which} \\ \text{?who} \end{Bmatrix}$ I can't read in the original Greek, is still to be found unopened on my bookshelves.

(37) Homer, $\begin{Bmatrix} \text{*which} \\ \text{who} \end{Bmatrix}$ I can't read in the original Greek, was a blind, wandering poet.

(38) The United States, $\begin{Bmatrix} \text{which} \\ \text{who} \end{Bmatrix}$ refused to negotiate last July, is now trying to reopen peace talks as quickly as possible.

(39) The United States, $\begin{Bmatrix} \text{which} \\ \text{*who} \end{Bmatrix}$ is extremely large in area, would no doubt refuse to allow India to colonize Alaska.

In sentences (40) and (41), a much more vivid sense of Capote as a person than of Homer as a person seems to influence my choice of pronoun:

(40) Sam can read Homer, $\begin{Bmatrix} \text{which} \\ \text{?who} \end{Bmatrix}$ does not have a pompous prose style.

(41) Evtushenko can read Capote, $\begin{Bmatrix} \text{?which} \\ \text{who} \end{Bmatrix}$ does not have a pompous prose style.

It often seems to be the case that other factors operate to lend an alternative, perhaps ridiculous interpretation to a sentence whose derivation contains two different applications of head deletions and a rule involving coreference, such sentences being either unacceptable or less acceptable than others whose derivations involve the same pair of head deletions and the same rule. For instance, speakers more readily accept (42a) than (42b), which in turn seems to be more acceptable than (42c). In (42a) and (42b), the words *reading* and *readers* force the correct interpretation, while (42c) could possibly mean that Proust wanted people to destroy his person.

(42a) Proust expected most readers to finish reading him.[3]
(42b) Proust expected most readers to finish him.
(42c) Proust expected most people to finish him.

Similarly, (43) is more acceptable than (44), probably because an alternative reading for (44), in which Genet himself is sitting on the shelf, is more likely than an analogous alternative reading for (43), the person Jean Genet being known to be alive (this knowledge aided by the present tense form *is*), and his name not being specified in the sentence as that of an author.

(43)   Because Proust was an illustrious homosexual novelist, he takes up a shelf of the Gay Liberation National Library.
(44) ?* Because Genet is a homosexual, he takes up a shelf of the Gay Liberation National Library.

Something even more complicated seems to be working in the next pair of sentences.

(45)   * If you keep playing with yourself, you'll fall off.
(46)   If you keep playing with yourself, you'll go limp forever.

In (46), the last occurrence of *you* is easily understood as resulting from

genital-deletion and not body-deletion, while in (45) (for which I hold
Robin Lakoff responsible) the second *you* can only be understood as
resulting from body-deletion. The unacceptability of (45) is probably
related to the unacceptability of (47):

(47)   * You'll fall off { your body }.
                         { yourself }

but just how it is related and how to explain the unacceptability of
either sentence is part of the problem at hand.

Postal has argued that lexical items are anaphoric islands with
respect to outbound anaphora involving both coreferential pronouns
and pronouns whose interpretation is identity of sense. He has also
argued that derivatives are anaphoric islands with respect to the same
phenomena. However, there are dialects different from Postal's which
often allow pronominalization of an NP forming part of a derivative
if the phonological form of the NP is close to the phonological form of
that the pronominalized NP would take if it were not pronominalized,
and such cases are given in (48–50). For some people, then, (48–50)
are acceptable, but (51) and (52) are not.

(48)   % Red-eyed people should conceal them with dark glasses.
(49)   % The best bearmeat comes from young ones.
(50)   % Football players should really own several of them.
(51)   * The best pork comes from young ones.
(52)   * Soccer players should really own several of them.

George Lakoff has pointed out to me that the presence or absence of
a command relationship is involved in judgments of acceptability about
sentences with invasions of anaphoric islands, since even people who
do not generally accept sentences like (48–50), in which the form to be
pronominalized is close to a phonological form contained in a derivative, will accept such sentences if the putative anaphoric island does
not command the pronoun in question, as is true in (52) and (54).

(53)   Joe Namath doesn't like football; in fact, he doesn't even own
       one.
(54)   Rich learned to speak Vietnamese soon after he was sent
       there.

Beheaded NP's are like parts of derivatives in Postal's analysis in
that in the derivation of a surface structure lexical item, an element
in the underlying semantic representation of an NP changes its posi-

tion and syntactic function in the derived structure of that NP. Beheaded NP's, of course, appear in surface structure as single lexical items, while a derivative as defined by Postal is a compound of some sort. I believe that a command relationship is at least involved in the relative acceptability of sentences in which beheaded NP's serve as antecedents of outbound anaphora, and if this is so, then beheaded NP's are like derivatives in this way too. However, although I feel intuitively that the following sentences, which are acceptable with varying degrees of enthusiasm by different people, are similar to those involving invasions of anaphoric islands, I have not been able to support this feeling with any evidence, since I have found no clear correlation between people who are lenient with regard to anaphoric island invasions and people who will accept any or all of sentences (55–58).

(55) % That church is full of cobwebs and dirt, but it preaches against impurities of the soul.
(56) % The hospital went on a picnic after it was repainted.
(57) % IBM went on strike today, so I'm going to sell mine.
(58) % Sanskrit will not meet today, but Japanese, which is an equally interesting language, will.

In any case, a study of the process by which underlying NP's are beheaded and a part of a fuller underlying structure comes to represent the underlying whole is pertinent to any study of derivatives and lexicalization in general.

Another closely related and very important problem concerning NP's resulting from head deletions is the problem of just which head NP's can be deleted. For instance, *IBM* can refer to an organization, a building, IBM stock or the price of it, various factions of the people that are on the IBM payroll, and conceivably even a bowling team, should members of that organization choose to form one. But what is the principle involved that does not allow the NP *IBM* in (59) to refer to all those who have in common the fact that they own IBM stock?

(59) IBM rejoiced at its high earnings.

And, finally, what NP's are to be derived from head deletions? For instance, is there any reason to posit fuller underlying structures and head deletions for all the NP's *Betty* in the sentences (60–64)?

(60) Betty is Jewish.
(61) Betty is attractive.

(62) Betty knows judo.

(63) Max thinks he's too small to satisfy Betty.

(64) Max thinks he's too poor to satisfy Betty.[4]

(65) Max admires Betty, and Betty admires Max.

This paper has examined problems arising from the interaction of syntactic processes involving stipulated coreference with a process by which surface structure NP's are related to fuller, semantically more explicit NP structures. In a theoretical framework in which syntactic rules relate semantic representations to surface structure, I have tried to find principles by which it might be predicted when two NP's beheaded by deletions of different underlying structures may or may not function as coreferential in derived structures with respect to pronominalization, relative clause formation, Equi NP Deletion and reflexivization. It has been shown that the coreference conditions are different for at least some of the syntactic processes discussed. Whatever the principles are that operate in acceptability judgments on sentences with "pseudo-coreferential" beheaded NP's, they are not describable purely in terms of surface structure facts, what syntactic rules are involved, and what underlying material has been deleted. The strongest generalization I can make is that the unacceptability of very many sentences of the type in question seems to be related to ambiguity; that is, many sentences of dubious acceptability seem to more readily lend themselves to an alternate interpretation. Such a generalization only restates the problem, however; what are the principles working in these sentences by which some alternate interpretations occur more readily than others? Although I have dealt with these questions in a generative semantics framework, the facts I have brought up present problems for any theory of grammar, and I know of no way in which any present theory could handle them.

APPENDIX A FOOTNOTES

* This paper was first published in 1972, in *Papers in Linguistics* 5:1. I first noticed the problem it is concerned with during a class in Ann Arbor, 1970. George Lakoff made me realize that I had noticed more than a random interesting fact, encouraged me to investigate it, and was also helpful in providing criticism of preliminary versions of this paper. It was he who suggested the term "beheaded." Andy Rogers and Larry Nessly were also helpful in their criticism and comments.

After writing this paper, I learned of Bolinger (1967c). In that article, Bolinger views the problem of what I call "beheaded NP's" as one of semantic elasticity rather than syntactic/semantic deletion; I now prefer his approach.

[1] The judgments about all the sentences in this paper are my own, although of course I have tried to choose examples that people tend to agree with me on. It has become

painfully evident to me that not only is it extremely difficult to isolate and describe the principles on which these judgments are based, but that people seem to differ in their judgments in bewildering and surprising ways.

[2] Fred Lupke and Georgia Green have independently suggested that the weakness in coreference conditions for pronominalization and relative clause formation may be related to the fact that these rules crucially involve a variable, while Equi and Reflexivization do not.

[3] David Gordon suggested (42a) and (42b) as a minimal pair.

[4] Andy Rogers first pointed out to me the difficulty of positing the correct underlying structure for the surface NP *Betty* in sentences like this one and (63). (63) is Postal's example.

Appendix **B**

What Are Clefts Good For?*

1. INTRODUCTION

Much of the linguistic discussion concerning the English cleft construction illustrated in (1) and (2) has been concerned with the proper underlying structure of this construction.[1]

(1) It's my rattlesnake that you should be worried about.
(2) It was only by forcing him to read the trash he printed that we could persuade him to be more careful about his editorial staff.

Attention paid to the communicative functions that this construction might serve has typically been limited to the discussion of sentence-internal relations like presupposition and focus, and theme and rheme, or to somewhat cursory observations about contrast or the distribution of new and old information within a text. In this paper, I depart from much previous practice in asking not "where do clefts come from?" but "what are clefts good for?", and in basing my answer on the study of clefts within particular discourses, most of which are examples of written expository English.

Following Bolinger (1972, 1977) and Gundel (1977), I assume that the introductory *it* of cleft sentences is referential, although the intended nature of this referent is clearly understood only as it is characterized by the relative-like subordinate clause that somewhat distantly follows. At least superficially, then, cleft structure suggests that the communicative point of a cleft sentence is the identification of a known referent, the element in predicate position (*my rattlesnake* and *by forcing him to read the trash he printed* in [1] and [2] above) functioning to identify the referent of the pronoun *it*. This is what in section 2 I call the "grammatical meaning" of cleft structure. While this grammatical meaning is the ostensible communicative point of any cleft sentence, it need not be the most important communicative function of this sentence within a particular context; various aspects of cleft structure and cleft meaning may be exploited for various other communicative purposes, since the grammatical form of cleft structure need not straightforwardly match imperative, assertive or questioning function.

In the sections following 2, I examine what the grammatical meaning of cleft structure is good for (section 3), what the linear and hierarchical organization of cleft structure is good for (section 4), and what purposes are served by the "marked" structure of a cleft (section 5). In most cases, my discussion is based on an examination of clefts I have found in the English of an informally selected sample of magazines, journal articles, and books, and the examples are taken from these sources.

2. THE GRAMMATICAL MEANING OF A CLEFT

Cleft sentences have as grammatical subject *it*, and as main verb the equational *be*. This means that most of the unpredictable lexical content of a cleft sentence is found in predicate position and in the subordinate clause that follows. In addition, there is an important logical and syntactic link between what is in predicate position and what is in the following subordinate clause: predicate position in the main clause of a cleft sentence always contains a constituent which completes a proposition represented in the subordinate clause. Thus every cleft sentence has an unclefted counterpart consisting of one less clause, in which a) the subordinate clause in the cleft forms the basic structure of the main clause and b) the constituent in predicate position in the cleft serves as an element in this clause. The uncleft counterparts of (1) and (2), for example, are (3) and (4):

(3) You should be worried about my rattlesnake.
(4) We could persuade him to be more careful about his editorial staff only by forcing him to read the trash he printed.

The initial *it* of a cleft sentence suggests the already known existence of a referent, although the degree of discoursal adequacy of *it* alone to refer to this referent is typically very low. This *it* is equated with (identified by) the element in predicate position, before the initial reference of *it* is clarified. The information needed to clarify the initial reference of *it* is given in the subordinate clause:[2] *it* refers to the previously unknown (or misidentified) filler of the logical role of a "missing" element in the subordinate clause. That is, *it* is equivalent to the logical role (agent, patient, means, time, etc.) in the subordinate clause that is actually filled by the element in predicate position in the main clause. In (1), for example, the vaguely referential *it* is equated with (identified by) *my rattlesnake,* but the initial reference of *it* is interpreted as the previously unknown (or wrongly identified) object that the hearer or reader should be worried about. In (2), *it* is equated with (identified by) *by forcing him to read the trash he printed,* but the reference of *it* is interpreted as the previously unknown means used to persuade someone to be more careful about his editorial staff.

This description of the organization of clefts is based on the assumption that the *it* of any cleft sentence is intended and understood as referential (c.f. Bolinger, 1972, 1977 and Gundel, 1977 for arguments to this effect). I assume this even though there are at least these difficulties with analyzing *it* as referential: a) *it* typically cannot be analyzed as a pronominalization of a particular preceding element; b) the *it* of a cleft cannot straightforwardly be regarded as a cataphoric reference to the subordinate clause as a whole (as can the *it* that accompanies extraposition); and c) there are difficulties with analyzing *it* in all clefts as a head noun, with the subordinate clause an extraposed relative on the order of the relative in the archaic-sounding *He speaks as a traitor who speaks of surrender* (c.f. Pinkham and Hankamer, 1977).

I ignore here the question of the underlying structure of clefts in a model of grammar which posits such underlying structures. My primary concern in this paper is with the surface form and linear organization of cleft sentences, and with the meaning and usefulness OF THIS FORM, regardless of its derivational origin or origins. My basic assumption is that in some linguistically significant sense we understand and use similarly, sentences that have superficially similar structure, even though similarity of surface structure may conceal important semantic and grammatical differences that have more traditionally been the concern of generative grammar; thus in my view the superficial equative form of clefts in English contributes to their meaning even though there may be arguments in a derivational model of grammar for a structure underlying some or all clefts which is *not* equational.[3] In this view the structure of every cleft sentence indicates that the communicative purpose of the cleft is to identify a known referent, no matter how quickly or exactly the audience for the cleft can be expected to grasp the nature of this reference, and no matter what other, perhaps more important, communicative functions are served by the cleft. This is what I call the central grammatical meaning of a cleft.

The proposition represented by the subordinate clause of a cleft is assumed to be true in its most general form, and what is asserted by cleft structure is the correct identification of a previously unidentified (and indefinite) element of this proposition. Pragmatically, then, we can speak of part of the cleft sentence as PRESUPPOSED (typically, this will be the entire subordinate clause) and part of the cleft as ASSERTED (typically, this will be the material in predicate position). Thus, although every cleft has an uncleffted counterpart which is truth functionally equivalent, cleft sentences differ from their uncleffted counterparts in what they suggest about a speaker/writer's view of the relative communicative importance of one part of a proposition versus another.

A distinction must be made between the constituent that syntactically occupies predicate position in cleft sentences and the element in this position that is pragmatically being asserted. The structure of cleft sentences suggests that what is in predicate position is of greater communicative importance than the low-content material that precedes it and the subordinated material that follows it; but this is not necessarily the same as the distinction between what is asserted to be true versus what is assumed to be true. Thus Gundel correctly observes that (6) (her 45a) is ambiguous with respect to what is being presupposed and what is being asserted:

(6) It was under the bed that we found the key.

In one possible use of (6), it is presupposed that this object is the bed. In another possible interpretation of (6), it is presupposed that we found the key somewhere, and it is asserted that where we found it was under the bed. Only in the latter reading does the syntactic focus completely match the pragmatic assertion; in the first reading, it is only *the bed,* that is the object of the preposition *under,* that is asserted, although the entire prepositional phrase *under the bed* occupies predicate position in the cleft.

Because of the grammatical importance given by clefting to the entire constituent in predicate position, we can speak of FOCUSSING part of a proposition in predicate position (henceforth, FOCUS position) and DEFOCUSSING the rest of the proposition in a subordinate clause. Quite naturally, grammatical focus is given to constituents containing information that is pragmatically asserted; but these constituents need not contain asserted information exclusively, particularly since in spoken English we also use stress to distinguish asserted content from presupposed content. (Thus in [6] we might stress *under,* indicating that *the bed* is being presupposed and that *under* is being asserted.) This kind of discrepancy between focussed and asserted elements in cleft sentences often occurs when an asserted element is part of a more complex syntactic structure, as in Gundel's reading of (6) in which the asserted element is the object of a prepositional phrase. In such cases, it is more accurate to speak of the material in the subordinate clause PLUS the non-asserted material in focus position as being presupposed.

3. WHAT THE GRAMMATICAL MEANING OF A CLEFT IS GOOD FOR

I have claimed that cleft sentences are structured so that the ostensible communicative point of the cleft is the identification of a referent. This referent is understood as the filler of the role of a previously unidentified element in a proposition which is assumed to be true, and this proposition is at least partially represented by the defocused clause. In accordance with their non-asserted status, the defocussed clauses in the texts I have looked at typically contain information which is not only presupposed in the sense of being assumed, rather than asserted, to be true, but also presupposed in the sense of representing information already shared by the reader. In fact, the information in the presupposed proposition is typically given or alluded to somewhere in the preceding text. However, it is also possible for writers to use defocussed clauses to introduce information not shared by the reader; an example of this is found in (7):

(7) It was a Vatican official who said last week, "The Holy Spirit operates in unfathomable ways, and maybe, through Pope John Paul's death, he was trying to tell us something." (*The Village Voice,* October 9, 1978, p. 34)

Here, the defocussed clause is being used to inform more than as background to equip the reader to understand the reference of *it* (although even here there is some justification for defocussing the clause on the grounds of being shared, since the suggestion that "the Spirit" might have had something in mind in the Pope's death is not new in the text and in fact is important to the article from which (7) was taken). Still, in spite of this introduction of new material in the defocussed clause in (7), the meaning of cleft structure is not countered in this example; it is at least plausible in this context to regard who said the rather long quote (that is, the identification of this referent) as of more interest than the actual content of the quote.

The grammatical meaning of a cleft can be manipulated for a number of different communicative effects, as long as this ostensible meaning is plausible, as it is in (7). Clefts can be used to avoid direct assertion of a proposition which the writer wants to convey without asserting, for instance; a possible example of this is (8a), which is taken from a book written for people preparing to take the high school equivalency examination.

(8a) It is through such practice that you will develop confidence. (GED Preparation for the high school equivalency examination, Contemporary Books, p. 309)

(8a) conveys something that its audience would presumably want to be true (that it will develop confidence), but it does not state this overtly as a claim about the result of using a product. Two unclefted variants of (8a) are (8b) and (8c):

(8b) You will develop confidence through such practice.
(8c) Through such practice, you will develop confidence.

(8b) and (8c) can be read as asserting that the user will develop confidence, while (8a) only assumes this, asserting rather the means to this goal (and further implying that this is the only means). In spite of the fact that the idea of developing confidence is being introduced for the first time in the next, it is plausible in this context, though perhaps sneaky, to treat as most important the identification of the way in which confidence is to be gained.

The two examples above are somewhat atypical, but not aberrant, cases of presupposition and defocussing in clefts not straightforwardly corresponding to information already shared by the reader. In both cases, it is plausible that identification of the focussed element should be of greater communicative interest to the reader than the information in the defocussed clause. What cannot be done by the use of a cleft is to clearly go against the meaning of cleft structure by presenting information in the defocussed clause which is undeniably more informative, WITHIN ITS DISCOURSE CONTEXT, than is the identification of the focussed element. Thus (9) would be a severely inappropriate way to begin a review of a single book, while this is not necessarily true of (10).

(9)　*It is in this volume that nine anthropologist-archaologists present a nutritious blend of provocative approaches to method and striking specific results. [compare *In this volume, nine. . .*]

(10)　It was in this volume that B.J. Smith first introduced a theory of universal packaging that was to influence the packaging world for several decades.

The relative acceptability of (10) is as it is because an author of a book review may plausibly view as of more interest the identification of the role of the book in a historic event than the fact of the event itself; but it is clearly ridiculous to assume, as the author would appear to be doing in (9), that the audience of a review of a single book would view as more informative than the content of the review, the fact that some of the content of the review is about that book.

For a particular cleft to be acceptable in a given context, then, the general proposition that is pragmatically presupposed must be of plausibly low communicative interest in relation to the identification of an appropriate completor of this proposition, but the information contained in the general proposition itself is not necessarily known to the reader or even, I would claim, treated as known to the reader. "Presupposed," when used with respect to cleft sentences, then, means "nonasserted" or "assumed to be true," and no more than that. The grammatical structure of a cleft shows the writer/speaker's view of the greater communicative importance of one element over another in a proposition, but the reason for this importance does not necessarily correspond to the prior awareness of the presupposed proposition on the part of the reader; writers and speakers may have other reasons than prior awareness on the part of a reader-hearer for defocussing a proposition.

The *it* of a cleft sentence implies a definite, unique referent. Since this *it* is to be understood as filling a logical role in the presupposed clause, cleft structure suggests exclusion of anything else that might fill this role. In this sense, all clefts which are not accompanied by a contradiction of such exclusion might be considered contrastive, in the same very broad sense that Bolinger (1961:87, quoted in Chafe, 1976:34) has suggested that every semantic peak is contrastive. In reaction to this broad use of the term *contrast,* Chafe suggests limiting the term to choice of one out of a limited set of candidates. Chafe quite accurately points out that clefts are often contrastive, in this strict sense; however, I believe that just as it is typical but not necessary for the presupposed clause in a cleft to contain information already known to the reader, it is typical but not necessary for the asserted material in a cleft to be in contrast. Contrast, then, is not a part of the grammatical meaning of a cleft, although the shape of a cleft is good for marking contrast. The following discussion is meant to support this claim.

I have suggested that cleft structure "means" that the ostensible communicative point of a cleft is the identification of a referent. Cleft sentences, then, are appropriate in contexts in which the identification of a referent is important, and in fact more important than the assertion of a proposition containing that referent. One such context is a case in which an author or a speaker is disputing the prior identification of a referent in a general proposition which is clearly not in question, as in (11):

(11) Andre Fontaine states . . . that the British shelled Damascus in 1975 in an attempt to drive French troops out of the city. This is simply not true. *It was the French who shelled the city.* . . (*Manchester Guardian Weekly* vol. 119, no. 15, October 8, 1978, p. 2)

In (11), clefting functions to substitute an alternative identification viewed as the only correct one, for another single and specific alternative which has previously been proposed as correct.[4] (11) is thus strongly contrastive: there is a maximally limited set of alternatives (two) and a choice of one of them accompanied by the specific exclusion of the other; in addition, the highly predictable defocussed clause does not at all distract from the informational focus given to the contrasted element.

The shape of a cleft is very good for the contrastive purpose of singling out one of a limited set of candidates to properly complete a proposition. However, the less limited the set of alternatives, and the less attention directed by the author/speaker to the uniqueness of the proffered completor, or to the nature and limits of the range of alternatives, the less contrastive is the effect of cleft structure. Example (12) below is still clearly contrastive, although not as emphatically so as (11), but it is less clear whether examples like (13) and (14) are contrastive in any but a very broad sense:

(12) Among the butterworts some enzymes . . . are secreted by the stalked glands whose sticky exudate captures the insect prey, but *it is the stalkless glands at the surface that furnish* the main outflow of digestive fluid. (*Scientific American,* February 1978, p. 112)

(13) Finally the membrane is plunged into another solvent, such as water, that rapidly precipitates all of the remaining polymer. *It is this quenching that forms the pores in the membrane,* as the rapid precipitation leads to the clumping or coagulation of the polymer. (*Scientific American,* July 1978, p. 112)

(14) This type of decision-making is difficult to reproduce in a computer program because it relies heavily on human judgment. *It is this difficulty, however, that makes the programming of poker an attractive problem to computer scientists.* (*Scientific American,* July 1978, p. 144)

In (12), *the stalkless glands at the surface* is clearly being contrasted with *the stalked glands,* and the contrast is additionally marked with *but;* as with (11), there is a minimal set of alternatives. In (13), however, and even in the larger passage of which (13) is a part, the range of alternatives is not clear.[5] In (14), there is even less question than in (13) of a range of possible candidates; the cleft in (14) simply underscores the noteworthiness and perhaps unexpectedness of the fact that the focussed element should complete the defocussed proposition, that is, of the fact that "this difficulty" should be what makes the programming of poker an attractive problem to a computer scientist. In both (13) and (14), unlike in the obviously contrastive (11) and (12), neither the adverb *only* (to indicate exclusion of all other alternatives) nor the adverb *rather* (to indicate rejection of a particular alternative or set of alternatives) would be appropriate to modify the focussed constituent. If any adverb were added to make explicit the reason for focussing, it would be *precisely, exactly,* or *just,* to underscore the correctness of the identification without a contrastive concern for specific alternatives. Most generally, then, what seems to be stressed in a cleft sentence is the remarkableness of the identification, and it is the larger context that determines the reason for this remarkableness. Typically, the identification is remarkable because it is contrastive, as in (11) and (12), or both contrastive and corrective, as in (11), but this need not be the case.

Finally, even the suggestion that the focussed element is uniquely appropriate to complete the defocussed proposition may be countered, as in (15):

    (15) It is with a great deal of pride that I accept this nomination. It is also with a great deal of gratitude.

I think it is fair to say that the cleft in (15) is in no sense contrastive; what is particularly unusual about (15) is its admission of alternatives. Although I think it is true that the *it* of a cleft sentence implies a unique referent, this implication can apparently be cancelled. The less the context suggests (or the meaning forces) the notion of choice among a limited set of alternatives and the exclusion of all or any of these alternatives, the less strong is the implication of uniqueness.

4. WHAT THE LINEAR AND HIERARCHICAL ORGANIZATION OF A CLEFT IS GOOD FOR

Clefts are structured so that the element in predicate (focus) position is the first (i.e. "leftmost") constituent that presents more lexical than grammatical content, and in the clefts I have examined, this lexical content typically contains some sort of "leftward" referential link to the immediately preceding sentence (and often to a larger section of immediately prior text, as well). Clefts are also structured so that the defocussed clause is at the end of the sentence, which is a good place for linking the sentence with following text; on the other hand, however, the presupposed nature of the defocussed clause naturally lends itself to recalling PRIOR text. Often, these three potentials of cleft structure are exploited simultaneously by a single use of a cleft; an example of such a case is presented in (16).

    (16) [introduction] . . .In the past few years my colleagues and I . . . have undertaken a different approach to fusion by inertial confinement. Instead of laser beams we have employed intense beams of electrons (and more recently ions) . . . [nine paragraphs later] . . .Lasers, however, have two serious disadvantages: They are inefficient and they tend to be expensive. . . . There is much debate as to the ideal wavelength for

a fusion laser, and a vigorous search is under way to develop efficient short-wavelength lasers. *It was primarily the inefficiency of lasers that led to the present interest in beams of electrons or ions as pellet igniters.*

The particle-beam approach to fusion has been made possible by the growth of pulsed-power technology, . . . (*Scientific American,* November 1978, p. 53)

(16) is taken from an article entitled "Fusion Power with Particle Beams;" the cleft ends a discussion of the disadvantages of lasers for igniting pellets. The focussed constituent looks backward, in that *the inefficiency of lasers* refers to the most important concern of immediately preceding discussion. The defocussed clause looks both backward and forward; it recalls the major topic of the article (fusion by means of particle beams), which has been introduced but has not been directly addressed since the introduction; and it recalls this topic for the purposes of development in the rest of the article. The cleft in (16) thus functions to reintroduce the major topic of the article after a fairly lengthy background discussion. Cleft structure is particularly appropriate for such a task, the subordinate nature of the defocussed clause being appropriate for factual material that recalls prior text, and the final, extraposed-like position of this clause being appropriate for setting the stage for following discussion. The cleft as a whole, then, integrates immediately prior text with more distantly prior material, thus marking the end of a large section of text, and it sets the stage for another section of text by reintroducing the major topic of the article: the particle-beam approach to fusion. A somewhat similar example occurs in (17):

(17) [beginning of article] Of all the measures dictated by the financial crises of recent years, reductions in Whitehall and local authority staffs have probably struck a chord of welcome in more hearts than any other. . .

[second paragraph] But there are exceptions, and the staff cuts in the Department of the Environment's Directorate of Historic Buildings and Ancient Monuments announced last October are one of them. . .

[sixth paragraph] And when the first survey at last covered the entire country in 1967 a resurvey was immediately begun. . .

[seventh paragraph] *It is this resurvey, now a decade old and still very far from complete, which will be hit by the DOE staff cuts*. And the effect will be most serious in the countryside because in recent years the resurvey has concentrated on the towns.

Thus by 1977 in Dorset none of the former rural districts had yet been resurveyed, . . . (Vole 9, 1978, p. 22)

(17) is similar to (16) in that the defocused clause both recalls an earlier topic (staff cuts) after a digression, and develops this topic to some extent (although here its development is limited to the following sentence). (17) is different from (16) in that the element in focus position, *this resurvey,* is not only tied referentially to immediately prior text but also plays an important role in a large section of following text. In this example, then, BOTH defocussed and focussed constituents have forward and backward ties. And this is understandable, in view of the mixed hierarchical and linear prominence of cleft sentences: In terms of purely hierarchical organization, the focussed constituent is most prominent in that it occupies predicate position in a main clause, and the defocussed clause is less prominent, being both subordinate and grammatically incomplete to varying degrees of severity. In hierarchical terms, then, focus position is a good "high-visibility" position for introducing a new topic. However, in terms of the linear organization of cleft sentences, the focussed constituent is in a better position to function as a low-profile, cohesive link with immediately prior text, and the defocussed clause is in a more prominent spot in that it is last, or "latest," a linear position which is often filled by sentential objects and extraposed clauses with relatively important content.

Any one or any combination of the linear and hierarchical characteristics of clefts outlined above can be exploited in a given instance. However, in the texts I have looked at, it is rare for some element in focus position NOT to share a reference with immediately prior text,[6] and it is rare for the defocussed clause NOT to recall more distantly prior text; in addition, I have not found an example of a defocussed clause performing a PURELY introductory function, except when it contains forward-looking metacommentary, as in (18):

(18) Many of the findings have already been incorporated into various machine strategies. It is to this part of our project, the programming of computers to play poker, that I should now like to turn. (*Scientific American,* July 1978, p. 147)

Most typically, cleft sentences put in focus position some element out of a set of elements mentioned or suggested in recently presented text, thus singling out that element as the proper identification of the completor of a proposition that has been established earlier as of some importance. Clefts are thus often used to recall a topic for the purposes of further development, or to "wrap up" a topic, depending on whether the defocussed clause is used as a foundation for further discussion or only as the presupposed part of a proposition that is finally being completed fully and accurately.

Cleft structure makes explicit the intended informational prominence of one element in a larger proposition. This feature of cleft structure is particularly useful in a discourse context in which the intended informational prominence would be likely to be misunderstood if the proposition were in unclefted form. I believe it is for this reason that it is rare for a focussed constituent not to contain an element that is bound referentially with immediately prior text, and for a defocussed clause not to recall more distantly prior text: on the one hand, focus position in a cleft sentence can rescue an element from what, in an unclefted variant, would be the relative obscurity of sentence-initial thematic position in a theme-rheme structure; and on the other hand, defocussed position in a cleft sentence can rescue from normally rhematic, sentence-final or predicate position, informational content that recalls previously given information and so should not be presented as new to the reader/listener. Clefting allows this hierarchical shifting to be done without disturbing the linear order that would otherwise occur if the proposition were in unclefted form; in the texts I have looked at, focus position is occupied overwhelmingly[7] by what would necessarily (in the case of subjects) or would probably (in the case of many prepositional phrases) occur in sentence initial position in an unclefted variant. Two examples of this kind of preservation of relative linear order with a reversal of informational prominence are given in (19) and (20).

(19) The photon gives up part of its energy to the electron, and the transaction is observed as a slight decrease in the frequency (or increase in the wavelength) of the radiation. Inverse Compton scattering is observed when a photon encounters a high-energy electron. Then it is the electron that loses energy to the photon. (*Scientific American,* August 1977, p. 38) [Compare: Then the electron loses energy to the photon.]

(20) Thus it may be that, far from traveling a road to extinction, at least the large kangaroos of the arid zone are thriving in spite of competition with man and the ruminant stock he has introduced. This is probably attributable to an extension of a suitable arid habitat. That extension, however, has simultaneously reduced the habitat suited to the kangaroos'

smaller relatives, the wallabies and the rat kangaroos. It is these marsupials that have largely disappeared from the interior of Australia. (*Scientific American,* August 1977, p. 89) [Compare: These marsupials have largely disappeared from the interior of Australia.]

In (19) and (20), the constituents in focus position (*the electron* in [19] and *these marsupials* in [20]) share a reference with a sentence-final element in the immediately preceding sentence, and in the unclefted variants of (19) and (20), these constituents would occur in sentence-initial position in juxtaposition with their coreferential "partners" in the preceding sentences. The most natural effect of this juxtaposition in (19), I believe, would be a narrative-like sequence of sentences, the second of which would be apparently intended as a description of what happens to the electron. The most natural effects of such a juxtaposition in (20), I believe, would be a misleading theme-rheme structure in the unclefted variant, with *these marsupials* being taken as topic and the point of the sentence being additional information about this topic. Without proper intonational help, non-clefted structure could thus be misleading as to the rhetorical function of the proposition involved.[8]

The examples below differ from the preceding two examples in that the relative linear order of an unclefted counterpart is reversed.

(21) The juxtaposition of other henges to causewayed enclosures . . . could have a similar explanation.
      It is with causewayed enclosures that stone axes from north-west England are often associated. (*Stone Circles,* by Aubrey Burl, Yale University Press, p. 25)

(22) Outgassing would have given rise to a secondary atmosphere composed of water vapor from the water of hydration of minerals, methane (CH_4), [the list goes on for four and a half more lines]. . . . *It is from this secondary atmosphere, the character of which was reducing rather than oxidizing, that life presumably arose.* As Haldane pointed out, the oxygen in the atmosphere today was put there mainly by the earliest living organisms, which succeeded in harnessing the energy of sunlight. . . . (*Scientific American,* September 1978, p. 73)

In (21), focus position seems to be used simply to get a constituent that is linked lexically to immediately prior material into a position where it can be linked linearly as well, thus providing a transition to a new topic which is introduced in the defocussed sentence-final clause. In (21), then, unlike (19) and (20), the linear structure of a cleft is exploited more than the hierarchical structure; *with causewayed enclosures* comes first because it serves as a transition, and *that stone axes . . .* comes last because it introduces a new topic, and the only other structures that would allow this order are marked for other purposes: the variants *?With causewayed enclosures, stone axes from north-west England are often associated* and *?With causewayed enclosures are often associated stone axes from north-west England* are both awkward, for reasons that I don't understand very well.

The singular appropriateness of a cleft in (22) is more difficult to appreciate. Unclefted structure with the same linear order, as exemplified in (23), would make a subtly different claim:[9]

(23) From this secondary atmosphere, the character of which was reducing rather than oxidizing, life presumably arose.

In (23), the scop of *presumably* includes only the proposition "life arose," which is not the intention of (22). In addition, "life presumably arose" would be foregrounded with no apparent purpose. But with unclefted structure and reversed linear order, as exemplified in (24), the cohesive effect of (21) is subtly weakened.

(24) Life presumably arose from this secondary atmosphere, the character of which was reducing rather than oxidizing.

(24), while not ungrammatical, does not participate as smoothly in the left-to-right flow which relies on the juxtaposition of similar final and initial elements.

(25) is a final example of a cleft sentence that is particularly well-suited to its purpose in a way that an unclefted variant would not be:

(25) SIR: What Alston Chase says may be true ("Skipping Through College," September *Atlantic*). Still, it is an elitist viewpoint that discounts one major strength of higher education in this country: A very high percentage of the populace is able to attend and perhaps graduate from US colleges. (*Atlantic Monthly*, November 1978)

Here, the most straightforward unclefted alternative is (26):[10]

(26) An elitist viewpoint discounts one major strength of higher education in this country:

But (26) gives no indication that *elitist* is being predicated of a viewpoint; rather, (26) is a predication about a viewpoint assumed to be elitist. A more accurate unclefted way of saying what the cleft in (25) says is (27):

(27) A viewpoint that discounts one major strength of higher education in this country is elitist:

However, the arrangement in (26) destroys the possibility of detailing the "major strength;" and yet another alternative, that of retaining the structure of (27) but postponing the predication "is elitist" until after the end of this explanation, would result in near unintelligibility. The best unclefted alternative is presented in (28):

(28){ A   } viewpoint is elitist that discounts one major strength of
     { The }
     our country:

(28) preserves both the logical and the linear relationships of the cleft in (25). It is not clear to me what else it does as well; but in any case it is not a straightforward unclefted alternative to (25).

In summary, then, clefts are useful in that the relative linear prominence of the focused constituent and the defocused clause does not match the relative hierarchical prominence of these two elements. The linear organization of a cleft can be exploited for left-to-right cohesive and transitional purposes, while the hierarchical organization often ensures that the left-to-right linear flow of information does not obscure the intended relative importance of elements strung out in left to right order. The hierarchical organization can also be exploited for transitional purposes, in that focus position can look forward with new topical content and the defocussed clause can look backward in recalling a more or less distant previous topic.

5. WHAT THE "MARKED" STRUCTURE OF A CLEFT IS GOOD FOR

Cleft sentence structure is "marked" in that the conditions for the appropriate use of this structure are highly context-dependent, and the structure itself is used much more rarely than are comparable unclefted sentence structures. The relative unusualness of cleft structure is good for indicating the relative prominence of the information carried by the cleft as a whole, within a larger text. In other words, cleft structure not only gives greater prominence to one element of a proposition with respect to the general proposition as a whole, by putting that element in focus position; cleft structure is also good for foregrounding the entire proposition with respect to surrounding discourse.[11] Accordingly, the clefts I have found in expository texts typically present and/or summarize information relatively important to the purpose of the text or section of text in which they are found.

In this sense, then, even the presupposed and defocused material in a cleft is foregrounded with respect to the rest of the text; although this material is not asserted as new, it is presented as important to the communicative purpose of the text. It is not at all unusual for the defocussed clauses of clefts in the magazine *Scientific American,* for example, to recall words or ideas presented in the titles and/or in the one- or two-sentence summary preceding the articles in which they are found; a glance at the *Scientific American* examples used so far in this paper shows that five out of eight are of this type, although they were chosen for other reasons. Three of these five are given in (29–31) below, with the titles (and, in the case of [31], part of the summary) of the articles in which they were found:

(29) (see [13]) It is this quenching that forms the pores in the membrane, . . . [from "Synthetic-Membrane Technology"]

(30) (see [14]) It is this difficulty, however, that makes the programming of poker an attractive problem to computer scientists. [from "Computer Poker"]

(31) (see [16]) It was primarily the inefficiency of lasers that led to the present interest in beams of electrons or ions as pellet igniters. [from "Fusion Power with Particle Beams," whose summary starts: *In one approach to controlled fusion a pellet of fuel is imploded by an external energy source.*]

Although these examples are from *Scientific American,* my impression is that they are not unusual in showing the topical importance of the defocussed clause of cleft sentences and the consequent importance of the identification which the cleft asserts. Given what I have already observed about the use of cleft sentences, this relative importance makes sense: it would probably be only a general proposition of high topical interest that a writer could effectively recall in the defocussed and presupposed part of a sentence whose main communicative focus is elsewhere.

6. CONCLUSION

My response to the question posed in the title of this paper has been based on the assumption that the form of a cleft sentence has a meaning which may be exploited for various pragmatic and rhetorical purposes, but which, in any particular case, will not normally be clearly inappropriate within its context. Briefly, this meaning is the identification of a definite referent whose initial reference *(it)* is clarified by the final subordinate clause.

The meaning of cleft structure is obviously related to what can occur in focus position of cleft sentences; given that the *it* of cleft structure is intended as referential, and that the asserted element in focus position serves to identify the referent of this *it,* the overwhelming preponderance of noun phrases and prepositional phrases in focus position is not surprising. Noun phrases are most typically used to refer, and English prepositions often accompany their noun phrase objects in syntactic positions where non-accompaniment would result in preposition stranding (for example the fronting of prepositional phrases in questions and relative clauses); in addition, prepositional phrases are often paired linguistically with concepts that we can view as thing-like, such as time (*in 1967,* for example), place (*under the bed,* for example) and manner (*with reluctance*). When noun phrases or prepositional phrases cannot plausibly be used to refer even in this loose sense, they are not cleftable, as in (32) and (33):[12]

(32)   *It was a spy that Mary was.
(33)   *It was by all indications that it was a good year.

A spy is predicative rather than referential in *Mary was a spy,* and I cannot think of any context in which *by all indications* could be viewed as referential. The requirement of referentiality, or at least of referential plausibility, is important for other constituent types as well. In (34–36), for example, the (b) sentences are clearly better than the (a) sentences.

(34a)   *It's that she's sneaky and underhanded that he says.
(34b)   (?) It was that she was so sneaky about it that bothered me the most.
(35a)   *It's destroy that letter that I did.
(35b)   ?It's destroy that letter that's the most important thing for us to do now.
(36a)   *It was flat that they hammered it.
(36b)   (?) It was scarlet that they painted it.

In (34a), the *that* clause is non-factive and proposition-like, while in (34b), the *that* clause is factive and would most naturally be a second reference to a proposition that can be treated as shared knowledge.[13] In the unclefted version of (35a), *destroy that letter* would have both the form and the function of a verb phrase, while in (36b), *destroy that letter* is equated with a nominal, *the most important thing for us to do.* The adjective *scarlet* in (36b) functions in other contexts as a nominal (and may in fact be functioning so here), but *flat* in (36a) has no corresponding nominal function and in this example its function is either adverbial or adjectival. Thus it can be seen that referentiality, or the plausibility of referentiality, is important for the acceptability of particular constituents in focus position.[14] I do not mean to imply that it is the only consideration, however; it is much less clear, for example, how all of the following differences in acceptability are related to referentiality, and I will not argue that they are.

(37a) *It was to apply that they invited her.
(37b) It was to annoy Jim that they invited her.
(38a) *It was although he had his glasses on that I recognized him.
(38b) It was even though he had his glasses on that I recognized him.[15]
(39a) It was unthinkingly that he accepted that offer.
(39b) ?It was rudely that he accepted that offer.
(39c) *It was quickly that he accepted that offer.
(40a) It's very often that you see those cars nowadays.
(40b) It's not very often that you see those cars nowadays.
(40c) It's very seldom that you see those cars nowadays.

Some of these examples are in fact misleading in their unacceptability out of context, but I will leave most of them undiscussed.

My primary concern in this paper has not been with the sentence-internal syntax and semantics of cleft sentences; rather, I have been concerned with the function of cleft structure and meaning within certain communicative contexts. I have found that the focussed identification of the introductory *it* is useful for contrastive purposes, but is not necessarily tied to contrast; that the defocussed clause serving to clarify the initial reference of *it* is useful for information known to the reader, but is not necessarily used in this way; that the in-some-ways contrary linear and hierarchical relationships of these two cleft parts are exploited in various ways for the purposes of directing the topical and informational flow of a text; and that the relative unusualness and complexity of cleft structure is useful for foregrounding the factual content that cleft sentences carry.

I would like to end with an observation about the usefulness of textual data for studies of non "basic" sentence structures, even those studies which are based primarily on intuitive data. Linguists whose primary orientation is that of generative grammar recognize that the appropriateness of the more "marked" sentence structures is particularly context dependent, and these linguists are also very inventive in thinking of SITUATIONS in which certain sentences might be spoken; but I think we often don't realize the limits on our abilities to imagine appropriate TEXTS in which certain less common structural types might function, and to imagine what kinds of discoursal settings might detract from or enhance the acceptability of a particular construction.[16] So, for a typical example of what I mean, I think Culicover (1977: 346) overstates the difficulty of getting -ly adverbs in focus position of cleft sentences; his example is found in (41), but it is like my example (39c).

(41) (Culicover's iv, note 3)
      *It was quickly that Mary climbed the tree.

(41) is certainly unacceptable; (42), however, is much better:

(42) (an author's response to this question: "Do you find it easy to conceive of and start a new work?") Ideas for novels come to me either with a great deal of difficulty and after a great deal of thought, or very suddenly, as if I were being handed a summons to write. *It was very quickly, for example, that I thought of the basis for One Sunday Afternoon,* although I didn't get around to writing it for several months.

It is not completely clear to me why the cleft in (42) is so much better than the one in (41), but I am sure that part of the reason is the cohesive tie of *very quickly* to the prior *very suddenly,* and the prior suggestion of a choice between two alternatives (slowly versus quickly), one of which cleft structure singles out in focus position—as well as the potential function of the subordinate clause as an introduction to a section of talk about *One Sunday Afternoon.* I believe that (42) is an example I could have invented only after getting a "feel" for clefts as they are used in expository discourse; and now I would not judge the acceptability of a particular type of construction in focus position of cleft sentences without construing the kind of contexts I believe clefts are used in, any more than I would conclude that a particular verb does not govern Passive, on the basis of examples like that in (43):

(43) ?* A chocolate-covered Bayer aspirin was taken by me.

It is well known that contextual factors affect the acceptability of particular instances of the passive construction. Readers will recognize that (43) is strange not because *take* doesn't govern Passive, but because of the strange final position of the pronoun together with an indefinite, "heavy" noun phrase in sentence-initial, subject position. However, the contextual factors influencing the acceptability of particular instances of other non-basic, marked construction types are less well known. I have tried to shed light on one of these other constructions in this paper.

APPENDIX B FOOTNOTES

*This paper was being typed in what I hoped would be final version when I read Prince (1978). The two papers are, in spirit and often in substance, similar; after the first shocks of recognition, it was encouraging to have another linguist, on the basis of different data, reach some of the same conclusions. This paper is substantially the same as that draft.

Many of the notes in this paper reflect the careful consideration that Ellen Prince and Robert Hetzron gave that draft. I am grateful to these colleagues for their insights. A full revision of this paper with Prince (1978) and Hetzron (1978) in mind would look considerably different, and I have not attempted to make one.

I am also grateful to Pete Becker, for comments and especially for his paper "The figure a sentence makes". I suspect that that paper may have started this one; certainly, my discussion of "the shape of a cleft" owes much to Becker (1977).

[1] See, for example, Akmajian (1970), Pinkham and Hankamer (1975), (Gundel 1977), Wirth (1978).

[2] I do not address in this paper the question of the exact grammatical status of this subordinate clause.

[3] This view has at least two difficulties, which I am not able to resolve: a) I do not know how to express the difference I feel between the equative function of a cleft and the equative function of "true" equational sentences such as "That is my dog" or "Sam is the culprit". Using a metaphor explored in Lawler (1979), cleft structure "mimics" equative structure; to me, this means that cleft sentences are dependent on the form-function relationship of "true" equative sentences for part of their own meaning, in a way that I am unable to express more clearly. b) This view entails the claim that cleft sentences and their uncleften counterparts differ in meaning, even when stress in the uncleften variant singles out the same constituent as asserted, as in pair below:

(ia) It's *you* I want.
(ib) I want *you*.

While this claim feels right to me, I find it difficult to defend. I thank Robert Hetzron (personal communication) for forcing me to acknowledge it.

[4] This kind of substitution is called *replacement* in Hetzron 1978. In that article, Hetzron presents a useful classification of what he calls *prominentis categories* (categories which are "elevated above the normal level of the sentence as far as communicational importance is concerned"); replacement is one of these categories.

[5] One might argue, however, that a curious and knowledgable reader might be considering various alternatives before reading this, given that it is clear from the preceding text that the formation of pores in certain synthetic membranes is important, but not clear how they are formed.

[6] "Immediately prior" most often means the immediately preceding sentence; but focus position in cleft sentences can also contain a summarizing reference to an immediately prior discourse unit. In (i), for example, "these lines" refers to the thrust of several immediately preceding pages of text:

> (i) It is along these lines, then, that we hope to be able to use our model of the universals in linguistic politeness to characterize the cross-cultural differences in ethos, the general tone of social interaction in different ways. (*Questions and Politness*, Esther N. Goody, ed., p. 258)

[7] but certainly not exclusively

[8] In (19), the cleft helps to define "inverse Compton scattering," which involves a reversal of the energy direction from photon to electron, by singling out *the electron* for contrast with *the photon*. Similarly, in (20), the cleft rescues *these marsupials* from a position of low informational prominence, for the purposes of contrast, but here the contrast is used to evaluate more precisely the idea that the marsupials of Australia are headed for extinction.

[9] Some cleft sentences with adverbials in focus position and the adverb-first unclefted counterparts of these sentences can even have different truth conditions, as Ellen Prince (personal communication) has pointed out to me with the following pair:

> (i) (John spent two years in Paris.)
> (ia) Then he met Mary. [= he met Mary later]
> (ib) It was then that he met Mary [= he met Mary during that time]

[10] John Lawler (personal communication) points out that this analysis perhaps mistakenly assumes that *it* in this sentence is not straightforwardly anaphoric, that is, that *it* does not refer to what Alston Chase says. In other words, this analysis assumes that the sentence in question does not mean "this is an elitist viewpoint which. . . ."

[11] I owe this distinction between focus (main informational salience in a sentence) and foregrounding (propositions which are central to the text as it develops) to Hopper (1976).

[12] Robert Hetzron (personal communication) notes that referentiality may not be involved in these judgments; rather, assuming that the subordinate clause in cleft sentences is presupposed to be true, the strangeness of both (32) and (33) can be attributed to deficiences of their subordinate clauses as presuppositional clauses: *Mary was* is too reduced in content to function as a presupposition, and *it was a good year* cannot serve as a presupposition for what causes it to be believed *(by all indications)*.

[13] Ellen Prince (personal communication) notes that the underlying object or subject nature of the focussed elements in (34) may also be involved; In (i) below, for example, a factive object is clefted with a much worse result than is a non-factive subject in (ii):

> (i)   ??It's that he shot her that he remembered.
> (ii)   It's that he shot her that seemed to be the most likely possibility.

My intuition is that what is most important is whether or not the focussed constituent represents shared knowledge and/or second reference; thus (iii) is noticeably better than (i), probably because it is easier to think of a context for (iii) in which "that he shot her" is one out of several previously mentioned facts that are being taken for granted.

> (iii) It's that he shot her that we must never forget.

[14] The question of the referentiality of *it,* on the one hand, and the question of the referentiality of the linguistic element that is asserted in focus position to be identical

to *it,* on the other, are obviously related. Bolinger (1972), in arguing for the referentiality of *it,* gives a number of examples similar to my (b) examples in (35–37) (and [38–41]), and has a characteristically insightful discussion of the reasons why they are better than examples that are similar grammatically but differ in their contextual appropriateness.

   [15] This example is adapted from Bolinger's example (162) (Bolinger, 1972:113).

   [16] Of the linguists whose work I am familiar with, the work of Dwight Bolinger is a notable exception, and Bolinger (1972) is an excellent example of the kind of sensitivity I am calling for. Pete Becker reminds me that a lot of people whose work I have ignored study texts, and have for a long time; thus to philologists, for example, the kind of admonishment I deliver here would be both insulting (to them) and embarrassing (to me).

References

Adams, D., Campbell, M.A., Cohen, V., Lovins, J., Maxwell, E., Nygren, C., and Reighard, J., eds. *Papers from the Seventh Regional Meeting of the Chicago Linguistic Society.* Chicago. 1971.

Akmajian, Adrian. "On Deriving Cleft Sentences From PseudoCleft Sentences." *Linguistic Inquiry.* Vol. 1, No. 2. 1970.

———. "The Two Rules of Raising in English." Read at the Winter Meeting of the Linguistic Society of America, San Diego, California, 1973.

Anderson, Stephen A., and Kiparsky, Paul, eds. *A Festschrift for Morris Halle.* Holt, Rinehart, Winston, 1971.

Andrews, Avery D. "Case Agreement of Predicate Modifiers in Ancient Greek." *Linguistic Inquiry.* Vol. 2, No. 2. 1971.

Austin, John L. "Truth." *Proceedings of the Aristotelian Society.* Suppl. Vol. 24. 1950.

Bach, Emmon. *Syntactic Theory.* New York: Holt, Rinehart and Winston, Inc., 1974.

Bailey, C.-J. N. and Shuy, Roger, eds. *New Ways of Analyzing Variation in English.* Washington, D.C.: Georgetown University Press, 1973.

Becker, A. L. "The Figure a Sentence Makes (An Interpretation of a Classical Malay Sentence)." Papers from the Symposium on Discourse and Syntax, UCLA, November 17 to 21, 1977.

Berman, Arlene. "A Constraint on Tough-Movement." In Corum *et al.* 1973.

———. "Adjectives and Adjective Complement Constructions in English." *Formal Linguistics.* Report NSF-29. Cambridge, Mass.: The Aiken Computation Laboratory, Harvard University, 1974a.

———. "Agent, Experiencer and Controllability." *Mathematical Linguistics and Automatic Translation.* Report MSF-24. Cambridge, Mass.: The Aiken Computation Laboratory, Harvard University, 1974a.

———. "Agent, Experiencer and Controllability." *Mathematical Linguistics and Automatic Translation.* Report MSF-24. Cambridge, Mass.: The Aiken Computation Laboratory, Harvard University, 1970.

———. "On the VSO Hypothesis." *Linguistic Inquiry.* Vol. 5, No. 1. 1974b.

Binnick, R.I., Davison, A., Green G., and Morgan, J.L., eds. *Papers from the Fifth Regional Meeting of the Chicago Linguistic Society.* Chicago. 1969.

Bolinger, Dweight L. "Adjectives in English: Attribution and Predication." *Lingua.* Vol. 18. 1967a.

———. "Apparent Constituents in Surface Structure." *Word.* Vol. 23, Nos. 1,2,3. 1967b.

———. "Contrastive Accent and Contrastive Stress," *Language.* Vol. 37, No. 1. 1961a.

———. "Entailment and the Meaning of Structures." *Glossa.* Vol. 2, No. 2. 1968.

———. "Essence and Accidence: English Analogs of Spanish SER-ESTAR." In *Kachru, et al.* 1973a.

———; *Generality, Gradience and the All-or-None.* s-Gravenhage: Moulton and Co., 1961b.

———. "A Look at Equations and Cleft Sentences." *Studies for Einer Haugan,* E.S. Pirchow et al., (ed.). The Hague: Mouton, 1972a.

———. *Meaning and Form.* New York: Longman, Inc., 1977.

———. "Objective and Subjective: Sentences without Performatives." *Linguistic Inquiry.* Vol. 4, No. 3. 1973b.

———. "The Sound of the Bell," *Kivung,* Vol. 2. No. 4. 1967c.

———. "Syntactic Blends and Other Matters." *Language.* Vol. 37, No. 3. 1961c.

———. *That's That.* 's-Gravenhage: Mouton and Co., 1972b.

Borkin, Ann. "Some Clausal Remnants with *as,* and the Equi vs. Raising Alternative." Read at the 1973 Annual Meeting of the Linguistic Society of America, San Diego, California, 1973a.

———. *"To be* and not *to be."* In Corum, et al. 1973b.

Bowers, Frederick. "English Complex Sentence Formation." *Journal of Linguistics.* 1968.

Bresnan, Joan W. "On Complementizers: Toward a Theory of Complement Types. *Foundations of Language.* Vol. 6, No. 3. 1970.

———. Theory of Complementation in Syntax. MIT Dissertation. 1972.

Campbell, M. A., Lindholm, J., Davison, A., Fischer, W., Furbee, L., Lovings, J., Maxwell, E., Reighard, J., and Straight, S., eds. *Papers from the Sixth Regional Meeting of the Chicago Linguistic Society.* 1970.

Cantrall, William R. *"As* V-ing Complements and Subject Raising." *Papers from the Michigan Linguistic Society Meeting.* October 1970.

Carrier, L. S. "Immediate and Mediate Perception." *Journal of Philosophy.* Vol. 66, No. 13. 1969.

Chafe, Wallace L. "Giveness, Contrastiveness, Definiteness, Subjects, Topics and Point of View." *Subject and Topic.* Charles N. Li (ed.). New York: Academic Press. 1976.

Chomsky, Noam. *Aspects of the Theory of Syntax.* Cambridge, Mass.: MIT Press, 1965.

———. "Conditions on Transformations." In Anderson and Kiparsky, eds. 1971.

Corum, C., Smith-Stark, T.C., Weiser, A., eds. *Papers from the Ninth Regional Meeting of the Chicago Linguistic Society.* Chicago, Ill. 1973.

Costa, Rachel. "Sequence of Tenses in *That*-Clauses." In Peranteau, *et al.,* eds. 1972.

Culicover, P. W. "Some Observations concerning Pseudo-Clefts." *Linguistic Analysis.* Vol. 3, No. 3. 1977.

Donellan, Keith S. "Reference and Definite Descriptions." In Steinberg and Jakobovits, eds. 1971.

Dowty, David R. *Studies in the Logic of Verb Aspect and Time Reference in English, Studies in Linguistics.* Report to NSF, Research Grant Number GS-32144. Austin, Texas. 1972a.

————. "Temporarily Restricted Adjectives." In John P. Kimball, ed. 1972b.

Ek, J. A. van. "A Grammatical Description of the Accusative with Infinitive and Related Structures in English." English Studies. Vol. XLVIII. 1967.

Elliot, Dale. "The Grammar of Emotive and Exclamatory Sentences in English." *Ohio State Working Papers in Linguistics*. Vol. 8. 1971.

Emonds, Joseph. "A Reformulation of Certain Syntactic Transformations." In Stanley Peters, ed. 1972.

Erades, P. "Points of Modern English Syntax." *English Studies*. Vol. XXXI, Nos. 2,4,5. 1950.

Fauconnier, Gilles. "Superlatives With Scope Ambiguities." Read at the 1973 Annual Meeting of the Linguistic Society of America, San Diego, California, 1974.

Fillmore, Charles. "The Position of Embedding Transformations in a Grammar." *Word*. Vol. 19. 1963.

Fillmore, Charles J. and Langendoan, D. Terence, eds. *Studies in Linguistic Semantics*. Holt, Rinehart, Winston, 1971.

Fujimura, O., ed. *Three Dimensions of Linguistics*. Tokyo: TEC Company, 1973.

Givon, Talmy. "Cause and Control: On the semantics of intra-personal manipulation." In Kimball, ed. 1975.

————. "Forward Implications, Backward Pre-Suppositions, and the Time Axis of Verbs." In Kimball, ed. 1972.

Green, Georgia M. *A Study in Pre-Lexical Syntax*. University of Chicago Ph.D. Dissertation. 1971b.

————. "Some Implications of an Interaction among Constraints." In Adams, *et al.*, eds. 1971a.

Gross, M., Halle, J. and Schutzenburger, M.-P. eds. *The Formal Analysis of Language: Proceedings of the First International Conference*. 's-Gravenhage: Mouton and Company, 1973.

Grossman, Robin, Jim San, and Tim Vance. *Papers from the Eleventh Regional Meeting of the Chicago Linguistic Society*. 1975.

Gundel, Jeanette K. "Where Do Cleft Sentences Come From?," *Language*. Vol. 53, No. 3. 1977.

Haas, W. "Rivalry Among Deep Structures." *Language*. Vol. 49, No. 2. 1973.

Halliday, M. A. K. "Notes on Transitivity and Theme in English." [Part 2.] *Journal of Linguistics*. Vol. 3. 1967.

Hanks, William F., Carol Hofbauer, and Paul R. Clyne, *Papers From the Fifteenth Regional Meeting of the Chicago Linguistic Society*. Chicago. 1979.

Hetzron, Robert. "The Presentative Movement or Why the Ideal World Order is V.S.O.P." *Word Order and Word Order Change*. Charles N. Li (ed.). Austin: University of Texas Press. 1975.

————. "Non-Applicability as a Test for Category Definitions." MS. 1978.

Hopper, Paul. "Focus and Aspect in Discourse Grammer," MS. 1976.

Huddleston, R. D. "Predicate Complement Constructions in English." *Lingua*. Vol. 23. 1969.

————. *The Sentence in Written English*. Cambridge, England: Cambridge University Press, 1971.

Hudson, R. A., *English Complex Sentences: An Introduction to Systemic Grammar*. Amsterdam: North Holland Publishing Company, 1971.

Ioup, Georgette. "Some Universals for Quantifier Scope." In Kimball, ed. 1973.

Jackendoff, Ray. *Semantic Interpretation in Generative Grammar*. Cambridge, Mass.: M.I.T. Press, 1972.

Jacobs, Roderick A. "Syntactic Compression and Semantic Change." In Corum, *et al.*, eds. 1973.

James, Deborah. "Another Look at, say, Some Grammatical Constraints on, oh, Inter- jections and Hesitations." In Corum, *et al.*, eds. 1973.

Jespersen, Otto. *A Modern English Grammar on Historical Principles* (reprint). London, England: Allen and Unwin, 1954.

Kachru, B. B., Lees, R. B., Malkiel, Y., Pietrangeli, A., and Saporta, S., eds. *Issues in Linguistics: Papers in Honor of Henry and Renee Kahane*. Urbana, Ill.: University of Illinois Press, 1973.

Karttunen, Lauri. "Implicative Verbs." *Language*. Vol. 47, No. 2. 1971a.

———. "On the Semantics of Complement Sentences." In Campbell, *et al.*, eds. 1970.

———. "Some Observations on Factivity." *Papers in Linguistics*. Vol. 4, No. 1. 1971b.

Katz, J. J. and Postal P. *An Integrated Theory of Linguistic Description*. Cambridge: MIT Press, 1964.

Kimball, John P. "The Modality of Conditionals—A Discussion of 'Possible and Must.' " In Kimball, ed. 1972.

Kimball, John P., ed. *Syntax and Semantics*. Vol. I. New York: Seminar Press, 1972.

———. *Syntax and Semantics*. Vol. II. New York: Seminar Press, 1973.

———. *Syntax and Semantics*. Vol. IV. New York: Seminar Press, 1975.

Kiparsky, Paul and Kiparsky, Carol. "Fact." In Steinberg and Jakobovits, eds. 1971.

Kruisinga, E., and Erades, P. A. *An English Grammar*. N. V. Groningen: P. Noordhoff, 1911.

Kuno, Susumo. "Functional Sentence Perspective: A Case Study from English and Jap- anese." *Linguistic Inquiry*. Vol. 3, No. 3. 1972.

———. "A Note on Subject Raising." *Linguistic Inquiry*. Vol. 9, No. 1. 1974.

Kuroda, S.-Y. "The Categorical and the Thetic Judgment." In *Foundations of Language*. Vol. 9. 1972.

Lakoff, George. "Fuzzy Grammar and the Performance/Competence Terminology Game." In Corum, *et al.*, eds. 1973.

———. *"Global Rules."* Language. Vol. 46, No. 3. 1970.

Lakoff, Robin T. *Abstract Syntax and Latin Complementation*. Cambridge: MIT Press, 1968.

———. "Passive Resistance." In Adams, *et al.*, eds. 1971.

———. "Review of *Progress in Linguistics,* ed. Manfred Bierwisch and Karl Erich Hei- dolph." *Language*. Vol. 49, No. 3. 1972.

Lawler, John. "Mimicry in Natural Language." In Hanks, *et al.*, eds. 1979.

———. "A Problem in Participatory Democracy." *Studies in Generative Semantics II*. 1971.

———. *Studies in English Generics*. University of Michigan Ph.D. dissertation. 1973.

Lees, R. B. *The Grammar of English Nominalizations*. 's-Gravenhage: Mouton and Co., 1960.

Lightfoot, David. "Indeterminacy in Syntax." In *Montreal Working Papers in Linguistics*. Vol. 1. Montreal, Canada, 1974.

Lindholm, James M. "Negative-raising and Sentence Pronominalization." In Binnick, *et al.* 1969.

Locke, Don. *Perception and Our Knowledge of the External World*. London, England: George Allen and Unwin, Ltd., 1967.

McCawley, James D. "English as a VSO Language." *Language*. Vol. 46, No. 2. 1970.

———. "Review of Noam Chomsky, *Studies in Semantics in Generative Grammar*." Available from the Indiana University Linguistics Club. 1973.

Menzel, Peter. *Propositions, Events and Actions*. In *The Syntax of Complementation*. UCLA Ph.D. thesis. 1969.

Meyer-Myklestad, J. *An Advanced English Grammar for Students and Teachers*. New York: St. Martin's Press, 1971.

Moravcsik, Julius and Suppes, Peter, eds. *Approaches to Natural Language: Proceedings of the 1970 Workshop on Grammar and Semantics.* 1971.

Partee, Barbara Hall. "On the Requirement that Transformations Preserve Meaning." In Fillmore and Laugendoen, eds. 1971a.

——. "The Semantics of Belief Sentences." In Moravesik and Suppes, eds. 1971b.

Peranteau, P., Levi, J. and Phares, G., eds. *Papers from the Eighth Regional Meeting of the Chicago Linguistic Society.* Chicago, 1972.

Perlmutter, David M. *Deep and Surface Constraints in Syntax.* New York: Holt, Rinehart and Winston, Inc., 1971.

Peters, Stanley, ed. *Goals of Linguistic Theory.* Englewood Cliffs: Prentice-Hall, Inc., 1972.

Pinkham, Jessie, and Jorge Hankamer. "Deep and Shallow Clefts." In Grossman, *et al.,* eds. Chicago. 1975.

Pope, Emily. *On Questions and Answers in English.* MIT Ph.D. dissertation. 1972.

Postal, Paul M. "Anaphoric Islands." In Binnick, *et al.,* eds. 1969.

——. "Arguments for Raising in Random Order." Unpublished paper. Yorktown Heights, N.Y.: Thomas J. Watson Research Center, 1970c.

——. *Cross-Over Phenomena.* New York: Holt, Rinehart and Winston, 1971.

——. "On Coreferential Complement Subject Deletion." *Linguistic Inquiry.* Vol. 1, No. 1. 1970b.

——. *On Raising: One Rule of English Grammar and Its Theoretical Implications.* Cambridge: MIT Press, 1974.

——. "On the Surface Verb *Remind.*" *Linguistic Inquiry.* Vol. 1, No. 1, 1970b.

Poutsma, H. *A Grammar of Late Modern English.* Groningen: P. Noordhoof, 1904.

Prince, Ellen F. "A Comparison of WH-Clefts and *it*-Clefts in Discourse." *Language.* Vol. 54, No. 4. 1978.

Quine, Willard Van Orman. *Word and Object.* Cambridge: MIT Press, 1960.

Reibel, David A. and Schane, Sanford A., eds. *Modern Studies in English.* Englewood Cliffs: Prentice-Hall, Inc. 1969.

Rogers, Andrew. "A Transderivational Constraint on Richard?" Paper read at the Tenth Regional Meeting of the Chicago Linguistic Society, Chicago, Illinois, 1974.

——. *Physical Perception Verbs in English: A Study in Lexical Relatedness.* UCLA Ph.D. Dissertation. 1973.

Rosenbaum, Peter S. *The Grammar of English Predicate Complement Constructions.* Cambridge: MIT Press, 1967.

Ross, John R. "A Fake NP Squish." In Bailey and Shuy, eds. 1973a.

——. "Adjectives as Noun Phrases." In Reibel and Schane, eds. 1969.

——. "The Category Squish: Endstation Haptwort." In Peranteau, *et al.,* eds. 1962a.

——. "Clause-Matiness." Talk given at the Chicago Linguistic Society, Nov. 31, 1972. 1972b.

——. *Constraints on Variables in Syntax.* MIT Dissertation. Available from the Indiana University Linguistics Club. 1967.

——. "Doubl-ing." *Linguistic Inquiry.* Vol. 3, No. 1. 1972.

——. "Nouniness." In O. Fujimura, ed. 1973b.

Schachter, Paul. "Focus and Relativization." *Language.* Vol. 49, No. 1. 1973.

Shopen, Tim. "Logical Equivalence is not Semantic Equivalence." In Peranteau, *et al.,* eds. 1972.

Silva, Georgette. "On Raising." *Stanford Occasional Papers in Linguistics.* Vol. 3. 1973.

Smith, Donald L. "Experiencer Deletion." Ms., University of Georgia. 1972.

Spears, Arthur K. "Complements of *Significant*-Class Predicates: A Study in the Semantics of Complementation." In Corum, *et al.,* eds. 1973.

Steinberg, Danny D. and Jakobovitz, Leon A. *Semantics: An Interdisciplinary Reader in Philosophy, Linguistics and Psychology.* Cambridge, England: Cambridge University Press, 1971.

Stockwell, Robert P., Schachter, Paul, Partee, Barbara Hall. *The Major Syntactic Structures of English.* New York: Holt, Rinehart and Winston, Inc., 1973.

Szamosi, Michael. "On the Unity of Subject Raising." In Corum, *et al.,* eds. 1973.

Wilkinson, Robert W. *Sentence Types and Complementation Types in English.* University of Illinois Ph.D. dissertation. 1971.

Wirth, Jessica R. "The Derivation of Cleft Sentences." *Glossa.* Vol. 12. 1979.

Zandvoort, R. W. *A Handbook of English Grammar.* London: Longmans, Green and Co., Ltd., 1957.

AUTHOR INDEX

SUBJECT INDEX